FRIEDRICH FROEBEL

A SELECTION FROM HIS WRITINGS

Cambridge Texts and Studies in Education

GENERAL EDITORS

A. C. F. BEALES
Professor of the History of Education, King's College, London

A. V. JUDGES
*Professor Emeritus of the History of Education,
King's College, London*

J. P. C. ROACH
*Professor of Education in the Institute of Education,
University of Sheffield*

IN THIS SERIES

H. C. Barnard: Fénelon on Education
Irene M. Lilley: Friedrich Froebel

FRIEDRICH FROEBEL

A SELECTION FROM HIS WRITINGS BY

IRENE M. LILLEY

Vice-Principal and Principal Lecturer in Education
Maria Grey College, Isleworth, Middlesex

CAMBRIDGE
AT THE UNIVERSITY PRESS
1967

Published by the Syndics of the Cambridge University Press
Bentley House, 200 Euston Road, London, N.W. 1
American Branch: 32 East 57th Street, New York, N.Y. 10022

Library of Congress Catalogue Card Number: 67–10990

Printed in Great Britain
at the University Printing House, Cambridge
(Brooke Crutchley, University Printer)

CONTENTS

ACKNOWLEDGEMENTS

I acknowledge with gratitude the encouragement and advice which I received from Miss Mildred Cant. I am indebted also to the librarian of the National Froebel Foundation, who made the Froebelian texts and other material available to me.

EDITOR'S NOTE

In making this selection of extracts from Froebel's writings and presenting an English version the greatest problem has been the form and length of the texts. Their meaning is locked up in a dense and difficult style, which resists translation in the sense of a full rendering of the original. I have therefore compressed statements and eliminated repetitions and digressions in an attempt to establish the main lines of thought and indicate those elements in his work which account for Froebel's enduring influence.

INTRODUCTION

1 *Froebel's Educational Ideas*

'You are occupied, I see, in the education of the people.' These were the first words spoken to Froebel by the Baroness von Marenholtz-Bülow, the woman who was to record the last years of his life and to publicise his teachings throughout western Europe. She went on to say, 'This is what is most needed in our time. Unless the people become other than they are, all the beautiful ideals of which we are now dreaming as practicable for the immediate future will not be realised.' To which Froebel replied, 'That is true but the "other people" will not come unless we educate them. Therefore we must be busy with the children.'[1]

The story of her first visits in 1849 to his institution at Liebenstein in Thuringia leaves an unforgettable impression of the old man who played with the children, the pied piper who drew them after him up the hill. He is the fatherly teacher who instructs the young women who come to learn his methods; they are grouped round him, listening reverently to obscure concepts with which they fill their notebooks, or they stream after him as he walks abroad when 'the contemplation of a stone or plant often led to profound outbursts upon the universe'.[2] At their first meeting he won the Baroness to his cause and, when she brought her influential friends to see his work, he moved them to comments such as, 'He speaks like a prophet,'[3] or, 'The man is actually something of a seer. He looks into the innermost nature of the child as no-one else has

[1] B. M. von Marenholtz-Bülow, *Reminiscences of Friedrich Froebel*, trans. M. Mann (1877), p. 2.   [2] Ibid. p. 5.   [3] Ibid. p. 19.

done.'[1] He delighted in evading the questions of those visitors who came to analyse and label his ideas. When two such critics considered that his theory echoed Fichte's idealistic philosophy and Hegel's dialectic method he said, 'It is both of these and yet it has nothing in common with either of them; it is the law which the contemplation of Nature has taught me and which I offer to children to guide them in their development.'[2] He was impatient with even the most devoted followers who struggled to define a Froebelian canon or to interpret his statements in practical and prosaic terms. They lauded him for his great revelation of childhood, but in the depth and manner of his thinking he eluded their understanding. In many respects he eludes us still.

Born in 1782 he had grown up in the period of early German romanticism when the main lines of his thought were established. On his death in 1852 it seemed as if his long effort to reform German education would be a failure, yet his educational doctrines were to exert a strong if indefinable influence in many countries, particularly in England and America. He inspired a new understanding of children's activities and ways of learning, and directed attention to their need for manifold experiences if they are to arrive at awareness of themselves and their world. He strove to show the significance of the child's earliest years and of his relation to mother and family. He saw that the young child needs a special environment in which to grow and learn and so he established the institution to which he gave the name Kindergarten. The value which he placed on a study of the child's intellectual and emotional growth stimulated

[1] B. M. von Marenholtz-Bülow, op. cit. p. 23.
[2] W. N. Hailmann, *Education of Man* (1887), p. 42 n.

others to more practical and precise work in this field. His interpretation of children's play and the outlets which he provided for it have encouraged further study and experiment. His thoughts about child and mother, family and school, derived from commitment to a distinctive and still challenging view of human life. The full message, which was elaborated in terms that have often made understanding and interpretation difficult, calls for a renewal of life in a new pattern, and the full significance of his insights into childhood is still being explored.

The wealth and nature of his writings contribute to the mystery. He seldom wrote in order to explain ideas in general terms. The outpouring of voluminous letters was a continuous monologue in which he developed and elaborated his beliefs. Almost all the works which he published were occasional pieces—pamphlets or letters which made specific appeals for support of his schemes, or articles which described particular aspects and details of his methods. Compilers and translators later on gave to his miscellaneous writings an ordered form which they did not in origin possess.

The difficulties of his style are to be seen in *The Education of Man*,[1] the most famous of his writings and the only major educational treatise he ever attempted. Characteristically, he left the book unfinished, since the task was vast and the form and discipline of such a text were alien to him. As with all his public statements, it was privately printed. It was never popular; one suspects that, though widely quoted, it is seldom read *in toto*. In all his writings there are formidable difficulties of presentation and meaning. His style is verbose,

[1] See below, pp. 176–7, for German texts and English translations.

repetitive, convoluted. There are long rhetorical passages, peculiar word-plays and eccentric emphases. He would never listen to criticism, or use the accepted philosophical terms. However, it is in *The Education of Man* that the main clues to Froebel's thought lie. The book contains both the ideas which he formed early in his career and the germinal points of his later discoveries in the field of young children's education. There is, in fact, a remarkable continuity in his work, for his basic assumptions, once established, were never altered. Moreover, although his doctrine was expressed in terms peculiar to him and may be repugnant in both form and content to those who do not accept his assumptions, it is a statement of an educational position derived from a perennial philosophy.

Froebel himself has left copious evidence of the influences which formed his thought, and this was done deliberately; he believed that observation and consciousness of the self were essential to the growth of every human being. Like the teacher in Novalis' novel, *The Novices of Saïs*, he set himself the task of revealing to others the secrets which he had learned in the course of his own development. 'The fundamental characteristics of my life from the very first have been unceasing self-contemplation, self-analysis and self-education, and they have remained so to this day.'[1] There are at least three major autobiographical statements which are, in effect, three different levels of analysis. In the *Letter to the Duke of Meiningen*[2] written in 1827 he justified himself as an educator by reflecting on the significance

[1] See below, p. 33.
[2] Text in W. Lange, *F. Fröbels gesammelte pädagogische Schriften* (1862), I, 32–118. Translation by E. Michaelis and H. K. Moore in *Autobiography of Friedrich Froebel* (1886), pp. 3–101.

of his experiences in childhood and youth and on the quality of his own apprenticeship to his vocation. A year later, when engaged in friendly controversy with the philosopher Krause,[1] he analysed the same experiences again in order to emphasise the main factors in his intellectual growth and to explain the germinations of his view of life. He went over the same ground yet again when he was involved in a deep emotional crisis. Having run away from the complexities of personal relationships within the small circle of Keilhau, he wrote from his solitude in Switzerland the most revealing of all his personal statements in the *Letter to the Women in Keilhau*,[2] in which he explored his awareness of human conflict and tension. As he reveals himself in this agonised appraisal of his personal struggle, Froebel is far more interesting as a human being, and therefore as a teacher, than the all-wise father-figure portrayed by his earnest admirers.

He constantly reflected on his own childhood and adolescence and sought to find those factors in the environment which impede or encourage personal growth. He found in his own early history much that was narrowing and repressive. The death of his mother when he was nine months old 'conditioned my whole future development'.[3] The first ten years of his life— 'the gloomy lowering dawn'—were spent in his father's parsonage at Oberweissbach, a village in the Thuringian forest.[4] Separated from his brothers by a wide difference in age, he was made wretched by the harsh indifference of a stepmother and the remoteness of a busy

[1] Text in Lange, op. cit. pp. 119–49. Translation of selected passages in *Autobiography*, pp. 104–25.
[2] B. Gumlich (1935), ed. *Friedrich Fröbel, Brief an die Frauen in Keilhau*.   [3] See below, p. 32.
[4] Michaelis and Moore, *Autobiography*, p. 9.

and formidable father whom he feared. Yet, although he was denied that membership of a close-knit family group which he regarded as supremely important, he acknowledged the joy of sharing in the work of a busy household and in the concerns of his father's calling as a Lutheran pastor. The 'old-fashioned, truly Christian life' of the parsonage, in particular the mystical and symbolic language of the hymns and sermons which he constantly heard, made an abiding impression on his cast of thought and mode of expression.[1] He interpreted his early experience primarily in terms of opportunities for self-expression given or denied to him as a result of personal relationships. This painful childhood was followed by five peaceful years in which he 'came to dream of life as a connected whole without contradictions'.[2] This was possible in his uncle's quiet clerical household at Stadilm, where he found the guidance of sympathetic adults and the companionship of school boys of his own age. There followed a period in adolescence which he always described in detail, since he regarded it as his apprenticeship to Nature. In fact, he was apprenticed from his fifteenth to his seventeenth years to a forester, but was mostly left on his own. If his analysis is correct, it was during this solitary period that his mind was set on the search for the laws and patterns of the outer world and its significance for men. He speaks of his 'religious communion with Nature'[3] at this time, and summed up the struggles of his early years in the words 'I looked within myself and to Nature for help'.[4]

The restless search for a vocation in the next seven-

[1] Michaelis and Moore, *Autobiography*, p. 7.
[2] Ibid. p. 104.
[3] Ibid. p. 25.
[4] Ibid. p. 109.

teen years or so was also his intellectual voyage of discovery. It begins with his journey to Jena University in 1799 and ends with the years at the Universities of Göttingen and Berlin and with the war of liberation. All his basic ideas were established in this period, though they were not reached in any orthodox academic fashion, since he had neither the preparation nor the aptitude for the wide course of study which he chose, and he made few social or intellectual contacts. He sought confirmation of the beliefs which he conceived, and was intent on something which no university curriculum could provide. He never stayed long at any of the three universities he attended, but tried his hand at many employments—land surveyor, estate manager, official in a forest department, private secretary, student of architecture, school teacher, tutor, and assistant in the Berlin mineralogical museum. Nevertheless, a constant purpose emerged as he became aware of his own capacities, and as he inevitably responded to the great movements of thought of his time.

'When I reached Jena I was seized by the stirring intellectual life of the place.'[1] At the turn of the century Jena had become the great capital of the German intellectual revolution. It was a centre of Kantian studies; Schelling had succeeded Fichte at the university, Schiller was lecturing there, and Goethe was near by at Weimar. Froebel says of the years between 1805 and 1810, 'Although I still always lived in isolation as to my personal inner life, yet I was at many points in full contact with the vigorous mental effort and activity of that stirring time, as regards teaching, philosophy, history, politics and natural science.'[2]

[1] Ibid. p. 28.
[2] Ibid. p. 110.

In spite of his fierce independence and pride in his self-education, Froebel obviously belongs to the age of his formative thought. He knew of the philosophic ideas then dominant, even though he refused to study or use them in any systematic way. He lived in the world of thought which Kant had made and he arrived at his basic ideas at the time when Kantian philosophy was under discussion and criticism by Fichte, Schelling and Hegel. Therefore, he regarded the human being as an organic unity and the human mind as a spontaneously active, formative agency. In his view, the mind functions by combining the manifold sensations of experience into a unity: the objects of sensory experience are intelligible not merely because the mind receives and associates them, but because it organises them into the unity of consciousness; and this is a constant process and a ceaseless interaction. This consciousness of the external world is also self-consciousness, for the environment and the self are in intrinsic relation. In Froebel's view the world within us and the world without are related in their modes of development, and there is an affinity between the mind of man and the course of Nature. So, throughout his life, the human being is engaged in developing his mind through the medium of the objects which he perceives and the quality of the response which he makes to them, and this response to experience is a total one, involving spirit, intellect, volition and emotions. The idea of an organic relation between subject and object and of a continuous process of development and interaction throughout the universe is fundamental to Froebel's educational thought.

His greatest debt to any one of the philosophers of his time was to Schelling. There is a danger in plotting

Froebel's thought too precisely, but he himself deliberately marked the chief points. He said that he was induced to read the works of Schelling by a young doctor of philosophy whom he had already met in Jena, and whose country estates he was surveying in 1803.[1] From their discussions he became familiar with the text of *Von der Weltseele* and of *Bruno oder über des natürliche und göttliche Prinzip der Dinge* and obviously derived much from Schelling's early philosophic views. In particular, his interpretation of the relationships between human beings and the external world was largely that of the *Naturphilosophie*. He saw a reciprocity between the self and the objects of its perception; as they are distinct entities this relationship is one of separateness, but as they have the same primary cause and the same essential character it is also one of identity. 'Nature is visible spirit; spirit is invisible Nature,' Schelling said.[2] Self and object do not exist in separate strata of being, but form component parts of a total reality, and the pattern of this reality is derived from God, for he infuses both subject and object, the world of the mind and the world of Nature. Everything flows from and returns to a common ground.

This concept of God undoubtedly presents some complexity of definition. It includes the first cause and active principle of everything in the universe; it is the being which affirms and realises itself in and through all things, which are its creations; it is the ultimate reality with which every living thing strives to be united and which is the purpose of every existence; yet it is also something which remains forever beyond the

[1] Michaelis and Moore, *Autobiography*, p. 40.
[2] Schelling, *Werke*, ed. M. Schröter (Munich, 1927–8), I, 706.

9

reach of the human mind and beyond representation in the material world. This God, who is both immanent and transcendent, is the beginning and end of all evolution.

In Froebel's system of thought everything is regarded as created with an inherent form and purpose, yet not as necessarily resulting in a predetermined style or pattern of growth. The purpose involves effort and struggle, since every individual being is striving to grow to its full development and to manifest its essential nature in a universe which is creative. The human being is perpetually striving to develop his capacity for experience, so as to ascend to higher levels of consciousness. The process of becoming self-conscious is a continuous effort, for it involves establishing relationships of increasing complexity with the external world and discovering one's own nature by becoming more deeply aware of one's own actions. But Froebel knew, as did others who held to this way of thinking, that the process of organic relationships is not one of ever advancing harmony, and the process of self-consciousness not one of effortless unfolding. He explained the obvious conflict and tension which creative growth involves in Schelling's terms of an underlying identity of opposites which, having a common ground, can be reconciled. 'Nothing comes without a struggle; opposing forces excite it and they find their equilibrium by degrees.'[1] He also uses phrases in which he attributes the growth of creative relationships to the appearance, within a situation where opposing forces confront each other, of a third factor which by its mediation resolves the tension and creates a new situation. 'Development is due', he says, 'to the reconciliation

[1] B. M. von Marenholtz-Bülow, op. cit. p. 3.

of opposites through the link of mediation.'[1] It is, however, futile to look in Froebel's theories for strict dialectical progression in Hegelian terms or, perhaps, to
pay too much attention to his emphasis on formal laws;
his phraseology was not intended to be philosophically
exact, though much of it was derived from terms in
common use.

Similarly, he used the scientific theories which he
found in vogue. Again, he has documented his sources.
At Jena his teacher in botany and natural history was
Batsch, who, he tells us, taught him 'that the skeleton
or bony framework of fishes, birds and men was one
and the same in plan' and showed him 'the mutual
relationship of all animals, extending like a network in
all directions'.[2] These were the accepted ideas of the
day. This was a period when the study of Nature was a
general philosophy rather than an exact science and,
here also, Schelling's early work provided some of the
assumptions from which scientific problems were
developed. The scientific giants in Froebel's world
were Goethe and Lorenz Oken, though he acknowledged their influence only indirectly and used their
concepts only as they suited his purpose. Biological
study was largely a search for the structural units on
which a classification of living things could be based
and for the constant factor in development which
persisted in the midst of incessant transformation—the
thread in the labyrinth of living shapes. Assuming that
lower and simpler forms of life appear earlier than the
more complex structures and that evolution proceeds
by constant rising to ever higher forms, the biologists

[1] E. Michaelis and H. K. Moore (ed.), *Froebel's Letters on the
Kindergarten* (1891), p. 298.
[2] Michaelis and Moore, *Autobiography*, p. 31.

sought for the unity of form within each species and for the vital force pulsing in all things which they deduced must exist.

Goethe, for instance, in his study of plant generation and organisation, thought of the parts of a plant as successive permutations of a basic leaf form. When he extended this concept of metamorphosis to all living beings, he looked for correspondences in the details of anatomical structure and strove to establish the basic types to which all the complex separate elements could be referred. This search for basic units led the naturalist Lorenz Oken—whose work otherwise must now be regarded as highly fantastical—to an intimation of the cell theory of organic structure. This search for the primal form, and this inquiry into the simple unities of pattern among all the variety of organisms, was probably the most fruitful scientific work of this time. When the total process of evolutionary ascent was regarded it was deduced that man, the last to appear, was the most highly organised species, the highest of living creatures. Such belief in the high rank and worth of human life gives a special glow to this whole period of thought.

Froebel believed that all living things are efficiently organised in that each possesses all that it requires in order to be able to exist and achieve total development under the conditions for which it is made. This is not a crude pre-formation hypothesis that each living being contains encased within it from the outset a perfect example of its species, which it lives to unfold. The purposes of growth were at that time more dynamically interpreted. It was believed that in every living thing there is a structural purpose, but that it includes an essential drive towards more intense and complex development. Also, evolution of species seemed to occur when a more highly organised variant of an existing species arose. This was a constant factor, for, it was deduced, all matter contains that which can cause change, since it includes forces both of attraction and of repulsion. Goethe's idea of the primal polarity of all beings, and Schelling's concept of a fundamental duality in Nature, did not refer to exclusive antagonisms, but to complementary interrelations. All things in the universe are connected and mutually responsive through attraction or repulsion. Both sorts of response are essential to the rhythm of life. In such speculations life was interpreted in terms of significant purpose and harmony; every living thing has evolved out of a primal form, develops according to an archetypal plan common to groups of other living things, exists in order to work out the special structural purpose which is from the outset contained within it, and is alive by virtue of the essential force which pulses throughout the universe.

Within the concepts and terminology of *Naturphilosophie* Froebel struggled to form his own version of the structure of the universe. Characteristically, he expressed this in mathematical terms. His thesis was developed in a treatise—*Sphaïra*—which was written during the first months of his stay at Göttingen university in 1811.[1] In this difficult and incomplete sketch he strove to find the basic form which of itself creates an

[1] See E. Spranger, 'Aus Friedrich Fröbels Gedankenwelt' (*Abhandlungen der Preussischen Akademie der Wissenschaften*, Berlin, 1939), pp. 16–19. Spranger makes use of an article by Maria Bode, 'Friedrich Fröbels Erziehungsidee und ihre Grundlage', published in *Zeitschrift für Geschichte der Erziehung und des Unterrichts*, Jahrgang xv, 1925, in which Froebel's manuscript treatise is analysed.

equilibrium within and between everything that exists. To him the sphere is the basic structural unit, the final form of the universe, and the symbol of the lawfulness and unity of the worlds of mind and Nature. God is the absolute centre-point from which everything emanates; he is also x, the unknown, and is therefore that which is sought by all and which is the sum of the positive and negative factors in any process of being. In their spherical constitution all things remain in connection; they each possess their own centre-point, and so retain the capacity for re-union in their essential being with the absolute centre of all. In the geometric forms of this universe the laws by which its dynamic force operates are primarily mathematical.

It was ideas of this sort which were important to Froebel at this stage. He says that he was unable to go on thinking about educational problems until he had solved for himself the form of man's development.[1] The solution now reached was for him final. It contained the premises of his educational arguments and the principles of interpretation which he brought to the problems of existence. So he maintained that the human being is in essential relationship with everything else, and that this relationship is expressed when, by his actions, he shows to himself the pattern of his mind or when he draws into himself the meaning of the world outside. Man teaches himself through the discovery of himself. He learns by living over the life of a thing in himself and coming to recognise its essence.

His main ideas were already formulated before he sought confirmation of them by inquiry into phenomena. In 1812 he went from Göttingen to Berlin expressly to study under Weiss, who was an authority

[1] Michaelis and Moore, *Autobiography*, p. 89.

on the science of crystallography; and this association was continued when he returned from a brief period of volunteer service in the war of liberation to become an assistant at the mineralogical museum. We can see why Froebel was attracted to this particular study and this particular teacher if we consider the implications of a treatise which Weiss published about this time on the various natural derivations of the system of crystallisation.[1] This work set out to establish a classification of crystalline forms through an analysis of axis and surface. Weiss traced back the manifold formations and variations of crystals to a primary structural unit—the sphere. Though recognising that the crystalline world presents no spherical form as such, he used the concept of a sphere to classify the progressive complexity of shapes, and showed that, the more complex its surface, the more closely does the crystal approximate to a sphere. Moreover, he used the concept of inherent spherical structure to explain the evolution of successive changes in crystals. In all this Weiss was following the usual methods of his day. Froebel, however, interpreted these findings as scientific proof of his theory of development. Throughout his writings the argument of analogy between the human and the crystalline worlds is to be found, and the distinctive feature of his version of the philosophy of Nature is its presentation in crystallographic and mathematical terms. They are, of course, not mathematical but mystical; the significance lies in the imagery and not in the formula.

The mode of Froebel's thought is neither philosophical nor scientific but mystical. His spherical law is a variant of an age-old theme. Although he developed the concept of the sphere with peculiar intensity, it was

[1] See E. Spranger, op. cit. pp. 19–21.

commonly used by the philosophic naturalists. Schelling and Oken, for instance, explained the structure and directive forces of the universe in terms of it. In general the roots of philosophical idealism run deep into the long history of metaphysical thought, and in the philosophy of Nature in particular there is a strong element of mathematical mysticism. Even so, the quality of Froebel's experience and the form of his understanding were more truly mystical than idealist. He relied on an intuitive unifying vision rather than deductive reasoning, and he reveals the character of his mystical experience in his views on Nature and God. A great illumination came when in 1804 he read the recently published works of Novalis, the poet and novelist of early German romanticism. 'The book laid before me the most secret emotions, perceptions, and intentions of my inmost soul, clear, open and vivid.'[1] In it I saw and found my 'innermost discoveries and thoughts expressed'.[2] The profound and disturbing impression was caused by his recognition in these writings of the explanation of ultimate reality and the approach to it which he had himself experienced. Here he found an intuitive response to Nature, a perception of the physical world as a manifestation of the spiritual, a 'mystical geometry', and an imagery of spiritual renewal and growth. Novalis saw Nature as a 'cipher writing' which is to be found everywhere—'in wings, eggshells, clouds and snow, in crystals and in stone formations, on ice-covered waters, on the inside and outside of mountains, of plants, beasts and men... or in iron filings round a magnet'.[3] It is a secret lan-

[1] Michaelis and Moore, *Autobiography*, p. 46.
[2] *Brief an die Frauen in Keilhau*, p. 32.
[3] Novalis, *Novices of Saïs*, trans. R. Manheim (New York, 1949), p. 3.

guage to which man has the key if he would but know it. 'We shall understand the world when we understand ourselves.'[1]

Another root which nourished Froebel's mind was the work of Jacob Boehme, the seventeenth-century Silesian mystic. His writings, kept alive by the mystical movement within German Protestantism, became of great significance in the period of Froebel's formative thought. Schelling and Novalis were among those who knew and used them, and Froebel himself eventually came to know all Boehme's works directly. It began when he was given the *Aurora* as a present in 1814, and years later he wrote from Switzerland, 'I still possess this book. It stands with the other works of Boehme in the room beyond.'[2] He himself records the powerful effect on him of this vision of living connection between the spiritual and the physical and of Nature as a symbolic expression of the unseen world.[3] His reading of Boehme stimulated Froebel to a wider use of the imagery in which he had already begun to express his educational ideas. Many of the Froebelian images were now evolved—the symbolic value of seed-corn, bud and plant; the special significance of the lily and the garden. In Boehme he could find ideas of reconciling union, of regeneration and transmutation of the self, and of an archetypal world in which the true forms of all created things are held to exist. Here he could see the mystical illumination which extends consciousness and a vision of the universe as the self-revelation of God. 'If', Boehme says, 'thou conceivest a small minute circle, as small as a grain of mustard seed, yet the Heart of

[1] Novalis, *Werke, Briefe, Dokumente*, ed. E. Wasmuth (Heidelberg, 1957): vol. III, *Fragmente*, pt. 2, p. 74.
[2] *Brief an die Frauen in Keilhau*, p. 71.
[3] Ibid. p. 100.

God is wholly and perfectly therein: and if thou art born in God, then there is, in thyself (in the circle of thy life), the whole Heart of God undivided.'[1] To this field of mystical experience belongs also Froebel's conception of Christ, who is both the historical manifestation of the divine in human form and the everlasting presence of divinity in the soul. Christ is the ideal human being and the model of human life, as he is also the mediator between God and man. Froebel's understanding of humanity is throughout illuminated by his sense of the spiritual reality of all beings and of the mediating elements which inhere in all personal relationships.

In his own story Froebel acknowledged another great influence, that of Pestalozzi. His indebtedness is apparent in his early educational work and can be seen in the more didactic sections of *The Education of Man* where he considers the elements of instruction. He could not fail to have been affected by the most challenging educator of his time, whose methods Fichte was then proclaiming as the starting point of national regeneration for Germany. He himself began his teaching as a disciple of the new method. Drawn into teaching by one of Pestalozzi's followers, he eventually stayed for the period 1808 to 1810 at the Yverdon institute. Undoubtedly he accepted the basic teaching procedures of Yverdon and in his own work exemplified the Pestalozzian principle of education according to Nature, regarding education as a fostering of all the potentialities inherent in a human being and as a process which must be rooted in natural relationships and conditions. He found the *Manual for Mothers*, which Pestalozzi and one of his followers had produced

[1] J. Boehme, *The Threefold Life of Man*, ed. G. W. Allen (London, 1909), p. 185.

in 1803 for the guidance of mothers of very young children, particularly stimulating, and some years afterwards started the observations which were to lead to his own distinctive methods, and eventually to result in the achievement of the Kindergarten. Yet he soon rejected discipleship, and his later reflections make clear that he realised a fundamental divergence of view and attitude. He did not, it is true, appreciate Pestalozzi's wide range of thought and immensity of aim. He saw only that he worked empirically, being concerned with man in his social rather than his cosmic significance. 'Pestalozzi takes man as existing only in his appearance on earth, but I take man in his eternal being, in his eternal existence.'[1] Pestalozzi had said, 'Man is my only book; on him and experience of him my philosophy is based.'[2] This Froebel could not accept. His deepest criticism of Yverdon was that, although each separate branch of instruction was efficient, there was no inner unity or interdependence, no absolutes such as his own idealism demanded. He and Pestalozzi were not merely of a different generation and background; the roots of their thinking were different. They belong to dissimilar disciplines and traditions.

Froebel believed that the educator's primary concern must be the growth of relationships. He saw no irreconcilable conflict between individual and society, for, in his view, life is everywhere manifested in separation and fusion, and is to be explained in terms of an inner organising principle rather than a mechanistic causal pattern. In Schelling's words, 'There is one fate for all things, one life, one death...There is but one world.'[3]

---

[1] *Brief an die Frauen in Keilhau*, p. 54.
[2] K. Silber, *Pestalozzi* (London, 1960), p. 92.
[3] Schelling, op. cit. III, 210.

Therefore, each individual is both autonomous and self-active and also bound in association with everything else in the great chain of being. The organic unity of the universe works efficiently at every point, and each part expresses in some sense the whole to which it belongs. This conception of the connection between the part or member and the whole, which was fairly generally accepted in his time, has a special significance for Froebel and occurs throughout his writings. He was fond of asserting that every single thing in life must be at once a whole in itself and a member of a whole, a part-whole. So the individual human being shares in and represents all the levels of the human community.

It was Froebel's hope that his view of life might prove the basis of a comprehensive educational system which would regenerate mankind. His loyalty to the idea of a German nation, first aroused by Fichte's *Addresses* and strengthened by his enthusiasm for Arndt, and his belief in education as a means of unification are obvious and constant features of his work. He believed that through his plans the whole German people would be united in a true community. *The Education of Man* belongs to the period when he laboured to extend the experiment at Keilhau into a scheme of related institutions, progressing from an elementary training in skills and activities to higher academic and technical education. The small school at Keilhau—the Universal German Educational Institution—which he started with the help of his two war-comrades, Middendorff and Langethal, was intended as a model for the nation, even as *The Education of Man*, which was the explanation of its methods and principles, was to be the textbook of the new education for

Germany and all mankind. There is no question here of an exclusive nationalism, for he saw a German nation as a part of the whole of mankind. Froebel was faithful to the vision of a regenerated Germany, and in his old age greeted the revolutionary year of 1848 as the springtime of the free German nation. In that year he presided over a meeting in his own state to petition the national assembly at Frankfurt for the general establishment of the Kindergarten as a first step in a national system, and meanwhile teachers elsewhere drew up a programme for 'the unity of German education from Kindergarten to high school'.[1] Even before the Prussian prohibition of Kindergartens three years later, there was always the danger of political persecution of his institutions in Germany as their wider intentions were suspected. At one time Froebel had even thought of joining the great German emigration to the United States and attempting to realise his ideal of the true German way of life in a new and freer world.[2] His aims were always vast and the institutions which he founded were only fragments of the original plans. Since none of his schemes was realised in its intention, the type of community he hoped a national elementary school might be must be seen in the small ventures which he fostered. In any case, size was not important to him; the seed-corn of the small living group was sufficient.

Keilhau was the centre of his educational work. Here he strove to realise his ideal of the unity of life, and here he established the circle of teachers and pupils whom he involved in the elaboration of his fundamental methods. It became the mother house as he created institutions elsewhere. When he pioneered two ventures

[1] See E. Hoffmann, *Fröbel. Ausgewählte Schriften* (1951), I, 175.
[2] See Lange, vol. I, pt. 2, pp. 550 *et seq.*

in Switzerland, he summoned leading members from the Keilhau circle to run them. When he left the Keilhau experiment behind and went on to the education of younger children, he regarded the Kindergarten centres where he worked as daughter houses and himself as head of the whole complex of institutions. Outside the Keilhau circle he came to rely on small dynamic groups for the dissemination of his ideas. Already in 1821 he had appealed for unions of women to advance the 'national work' of German education and, in later years, receiving no official support from any of the states, he repeatedly asked for the creation of neighbourhood groups to initiate the new principles. He called on German women to join in setting up local Kindergartens,[1] and on German men to found educational unions which would start the urgent task of improving infant education as a preliminary to general reform.[2] The success of the Kindergarten movement in his lifetime derived from the vitality of such small groups. He demanded from himself and his followers tireless service and entire commitment. His letters, which are part of his educational testament, reveal the tensions and achievements of the men and women of the Keilhau group, the circle closest to him, and they also enlarge our knowledge of the level of personal development and response which he demanded.[3]

His unitive ideal of life required that men and women make their distinctive contributions to the work of family and school, but it also acknowledged the tension of polarity in human association and the conflict in the

[1] See below, p. 117.
[2] E. Hoffmann, op. cit. 1, 126–8 ('Aufruf an die deutschen Männer', 1845).
[3] See Hoffmann, op. cit. 1, 187–8, for a list of the letters printed at various times between 1860 and 1948.

response of men and women to each other. He was well aware of impediments in the way of personal knowledge and communication. During the most formative years of his thought he was deeply involved in a spiritual marriage, as he called it, with Caroline von Holzhausen, the mother of the Frankfurt pupils whom he tutored. It was from the frustration and claims of this association, which he came to find oppressive, that he fled to Göttingen, but he did not free himself from the 'iron chains' until, years afterwards, he traced the course of their deep attachment and gradual estrangement in the *Letter to the Women in Keilhau*.[1] In this remarkable self-analysis he tried also to make his wife and the other women who were of the Keilhau circle understand him and his relationship to themselves. He was, indeed, conscious that personal growth and integration are a struggle and that response to other human beings, which may be conditioned in the earliest years of life, is a most delicate growth.

In Froebel's view the human being is always in relationship and every association is formative. The educator, therefore, needs to be highly conscious of his own intentions and actions and finely sensitive to the child's total needs. Moreover, the parent or teacher is inevitably involved with the child in the processes of learning and growth. As Froebel considered that for every individual there is an eternal complete form, so he regarded it as highly important that the child should be guided in his finite existence, in order that his development may be true to the stages of growth. Therefore, he saw adult guidance in terms of recognition of the growing points in the young life and provision of the means by which each phase may be fulfilled.

[1] *Brief an die Frauen in Keilhau*, pp. 55–9.

In his instructions to parents and Kindergartners Froebel told them to be aware of their own life from its early stages, to search into the child's life so as to establish its present phase of development and its requirements, and to examine the child's environment in order to see how far it meets his needs. In his writings he shows how the first important connection of the child with the mother widens out from family and school into the great complex of human communities, and he insists that, since human beings do not confront each other as isolated units, these are real connections founded in a single spiritual reality. Furthermore, as the earliest stages of growth are the most important, so the first association is the most formative and the bonds which the individual establishes with his surroundings at this time are of vital significance for his growth.

'Let my aim be to give man himself,' Froebel declared.[1] Since man's purpose is to know himself and the aim of education must therefore be the development of this self-consciousness, it is desirable to establish how this is achieved. 'The child must first see and grasp his own life in an objective manifestation before he can know and understand it in himself.'[2] He learns to know his surroundings, the shape, texture and function of things, as he acts upon them in ways which are natural to him. For the young child this means of activity is play, the purpose of which is given as 'to guide children back upon their own nature' and 'to lead them onward to observe the life of the outer world'.[3] For the older child the means are the practical

---

[1] Michaelis and Moore, *Autobiography*, p. 49.
[2] See below, p. 110.
[3] Michaelis and Moore, *Letters*, p. 92.

skills and occupations such as Froebel had already developed in the Keilhau household. To the child the adult world of parent and teacher is important, for, without their support, he may be slow to start the ascent from the diversity of sensory experience to the unity of self-consciousness and, without their guidance, he may not be able to release his essential self or read the secret writing of the outer world.

2 *The Froebelian Movement*

To his great disappointment the influence of Froebel's work was limited in Germany, especially after the prohibition of the Kindergarten in Prussia in the year before his death. Its immediate future, therefore, was in the hands of individuals. Devoted disciples and trained Kindergartners spread the institution of the Kindergarten in western Europe and the U.S.A. Missioners, chief among whom was the Baroness Bertha von Marenholtz-Bülow, made converts and undertook to explain and interpret the basic principles in speeches and writings. Institutions, such as the Pestalozzi-Froebel House set up in Berlin by Froebel's grand-niece in 1881, became influential centres where the creative ideas were given expression in new forms. In England the movement began in 1854 when the first group of Froebelians came over and began to make converts. It started to prosper and to have an effect on elementary school methods in the 1870s. The Froebel Society, established in 1874, pioneered with the training of teachers skilled in knowledge of children, and became the centre of the movement which influenced educational thought generally and brought into the field of public education that concern for young children which eventually transformed the infant schools. As members of organised groups committed to the statement of a specific theory and the promotion of a specialised institution, the Froebelians, especially in the U.S.A. and Great Britain, made remarkable advances in the second part of the nineteenth century.

Yet Froebel had with Messianic fervour proclaimed the need for a 'renewal of life' and a transformation of society, and his most perceptive followers, not content to write Kindergarten manuals and use the stereotyped games and apparatus, endeavoured to penetrate the State systems of national education. In England a remarkable success was achieved, in so far as Kindergarten exercises and games became a recognised feature of infant schools by the end of the century, but this ground was won only after long struggle and at the cost of the great ideals of organic growth and unity and the respect and love for children's real nature which Froebel proclaimed. For a long time the Froebelian movement was dominated by an interpretation of the principles which tied it to the rigid pedagogical system of the Kindergarten.

In England the movement was rescued from this atrophy as the Froebelians themselves turned to the larger study of Froebel's work and to an interpretation which related it to the scientific, sociological and psychological ideas which were at the turn of the century affecting all educational theory and practice. In the U.S.A., where public as well as private Kindergartens had been set up, the movement had long shown a greater sympathy for the transcendental and symbolic features of Froebel's teaching. In both countries, however, a new phase opened up as the study of children's behaviour and concepts developed. In this respect,

Dewey, the most sympathetic and authoritative inter-
preter of Froebelian pedagogy at this time, was the
severest critic of both the symbolism and the discipline
of games and exercises. From this point Froebelians
returned to the study of children's nature and relationships and, in abandoning the formalism of the Kindergarten, found again the meaning of Froebel's 'renewal
of life', and entered a wider though less defined field of
influence.

3 Texts, Translations, and Major Critiques

Although in the early period his methods were treated
as final revelations of the only true way of teaching
young children, Froebel's words on the general purposes of life and education remained largely unread.
One of the most influential leaders of the English
movement even doubted the wisdom of translating the
texts, fearing that they were too alien in thought to help
the advance of the ideas in this country.[1] Even when
they became more widely known at the turn of the
century, the tendency was to emphasise the observations on children's behaviour and phases of growth and
to reject the mystical and the symbolic.

The texts[2] were not accessible even in the original
until Wichard Lange made a selection of the chief
works and published them in 1862–3 in three volumes.
This remained the standard source until fairly recently,
since it was not superseded by a very similar collection
made by Friedrich Seidel twenty years later. One of the
results of Lange's work was a persistent tendency to

[1] Emily A. E. Shirreff, *The Kindergarten* (London, 1880), p.
109.
[2] See below, pp. 176–7, for texts and translations and for the
major critical works in English.

rearrange the writings into a more ordered pattern, so that miscellaneous lectures and articles regarding the later work were presented as a complete theme, and to impose on the principal text, *The Education of Man*, a division into main sections and numbered paragraphs which were not in the original. Indeed, the character of Froebel's writings necessitates the imposition of some sort of organisation.

Translation and presentation of any of these writings involve serious difficulties, and for some time they continued to be inaccessible to most English-speaking Froebelians. Two American translations of *The Education of Man* opened the way to an understanding. The first, by Josephine Jarvis, is the most literal and least intelligible of the versions. The other, by W. N. Hailmann, is likely to remain the most useful and faithfully accurate translation of almost the entire work. The only two versions published in England were adaptations. William Herford's *The Student's Froebel*, which appeared in two parts in 1893–4, is certainly the most lively presentation of very many important sections and includes summaries of the Kindergarten writings, but, since quite half the work is taken up with the author's explanatory interpolations, it is also more subjective and even eccentric than the others. In 1912 the version by S. S. F. Fletcher and J. Welton—*Froebel's Chief Writings on Education*—was published. This is the most useful and lucid, for it aimed at expressing and explaining the basic thought, and so it tends to give the writings a precision of organisation which they do not possess.

Froebel's works have suffered from lack of serious analysis and criticism as well as from their obscurity and inaccessibility. Early interpreters, especially the

Baroness, intensified the idealist basis and dialectical pattern of Froebel's thought, and justified the Kindergarten methods and universal 'laws' of development in markedly Hegelian terms. Another attempt was made early in this century by the American MacVannel and others to establish Froebel as an educational philosopher by tracing the antecedents of his thought, but the onslaught made by the pragmatist Kilpatrick on the entire philosophical position hardly permitted the argument to be taken any further in these terms. In England Graham Wallas was the first really formidable critic of Froebelian theory, which he attacked on the ground that it did not stress the significance of man's social environment as the determinant of his growth as an individual. Wallas was the first to explain that Froebel's thought was rooted in the transcendental biology of his day and therefore for a time to compel assessment of it in these terms.

The reappraisal of the theories in psychological terms fared better. In England the movement was rescued from its attachment to associationist theories, which had been adopted as an explanation of the sensory training of the Kindergarten, and restored to the concept of the unity and continuity of psychic life by the efforts of E. R. Murray. The theory of play was reinterpreted so as to shed the symbolism and the pedagogic direction, and to relate to developing knowledge of both its biological and its psychological function. Recently the centenary of Froebel's death stimulated more profound assessments of his educational significance in the book *Friedrich Froebel and English Education*, edited by Dr Evelyn Lawrence, and in Professor Judges' lecture on *Freedom: Froebel's Vision and our Reality*, which moved the discussion on to new ground. Also, it is in the last half-century, especially as publication of the original writings has increased, that serious consideration has first been given to the theories by German authors, and here Eduard Spranger's article *Aus Friedrich Fröbels Gedankenwelt* must be central to any consideration of the genesis and significance of the ideas. It remains important to assess these ideas in the terms in which they were stated. Froebel's insight into human life and purpose derived from a mystical experience and an idealist pattern of thought. However alien the mode of expression may be to us now, his work shows a remarkable understanding of the cultivation of self-awareness and the growth and character of personal and social relationships which are important factors in education.

I VOCATION

Froebel has described in several versions the events and impressions of his early life and his choice of the vocation of teaching. In the gradual discovery of his calling he saw two turning points. One came in 1806–7 when, after his first experience in a school and his first visit to Pestalozzi, he reached the decision that he would abandon a promising career as a schoolteacher and the hope of proceeding again to a university and become a private tutor to the sons of Caroline von Holzhausen. The other came in 1816 when he had fulfilled his ambitions of a university education and was working in the mineralogical museum in Berlin. He decided to found a school of his own, to which he gave the title of Universal German Educational Institution. Important factors in this decision were his hopes for a united and transformed Germany, his assurance of the participation in such a venture of fellow students with whom he had campaigned in 1813–14, and his sense of obligation to educate the sons of his brothers and return to his own native state.

During the early years of this institution which was established at Keilhau, a little village in Schwarzburg-Rudolstadt, he wrote many articles on its aims and methods, some of which were published in the journal *Isis*. In 1823 the philosopher Krause commented in the same journal on the articles, declaring his basic agreement with the principles, but criticising the phrase 'Universal German' as a contradiction in terms. Froebel's answer to the criticism came in a long autobiographical letter to Krause which, however, was not written until five years later, at a time when the flourishing institution at Keilhau had been badly hit in a wave of political reaction and its liberal and nationalist tone had earned it the name of 'a nest of demagogues'.[1] Although Froebel defended the position taken up in the title of his institution, he shows in this letter his acceptance

[1] E. Hoffmann, op. cit. I, 161.

31

of the fact that it was premature to talk of German education as a system which would be universally valid.

Three years after the Krause letter he looked back again at the complex of thoughts and feelings which had led him to start the Keilhau venture. In another long letter—the *Letter to the Women in Keilhau*—he attempted an explanation of the vision of the educator's vocation which had come to him in 1816. His definition here shows the effect of his growing interest in symbolism; in setting down his reflections on the seal devised for Keilhau, he stressed the significance to him of the pattern of a trinity and the form of the ring or sphere. This mode of thought was eventually to be expressed in the playthings which he devised for young children in the Kindergarten and which were symbolic statements of the growing consciousness which, in his view, the child had of the nature of the universe.

1   Letter to the Duke of Meiningen (*1827*)

W. Lange, *Friedrich Fröbels gesammelte pädagogische Schriften,* vol. i, pt. i, pp. 32, 38, 87–91, 95–6

I was born on 21 April 1782 at Oberweissbach in the Thuringian Forest. My father, who died in 1802, was the leading clergyman there. I was at an early age initiated into the pain and pressure of life's conflict, and was affected by unnatural circumstances and an unsatisfactory education. Soon after my birth my mother became ill, and she died after she had nursed me for nine months. The shock of this loss conditioned my whole future development and this event, I consider, more or less determined the circumstances of my life...

My father, as I have already mentioned, was of the old orthodox school of theology, and so the language of hymns and sermons was strongly metaphorical and symbolic—a stone language, as it were, for it takes a powerful disruptive force to break its outer covering and release the inner meaning. This may be hidden even from a mature mind at the height of its powers; yet a young person in his first exploration of cause and connection can often grasp it, though the period of experiment and reflection may well be prolonged. I was, indeed, delighted if ever my searchings led me to find a meaning.

I grew up in early childhood among surroundings which gave me many sensory experiences, and so from the first I paid close attention to the pleasures which the senses provide. It was my habit to analyse and question, and my conclusions were quite clear and positive even if they were not put into words. I realised that sensory pleasures are transitory, without any enduring or satisfying influence, and so should never be pursued too seriously. I was at that time entirely impressed with this conviction, just as now I base the whole foundation of my life for the future on a critical examination and comparison of the inner and outer worlds and on a study of their interconnection. The fundamental characteristics of my life from the very first have been unceasing self-contemplation, self-analysis and self-education, and they have remained so to this day.

In my educational work it has always been my fundamental principle and aim that the human being's pleasure and power in working uninterruptedly at his own education should be aroused and strengthened...

I entered my new sphere of educational work in July 1807. I was twenty-five years of age but still immature. I was conscious not of my age but of my ambition, of my whole intellectual development and experience. I knew that I was awkward and uneducated, ignorant of life both as it is and as it seems to be. My whole up-bringing could only lead me into conflict, for from now on I found myself at odds with all existing forms of education, and so the whole of my teaching and tutorial career was one long battle.

It was good for me that this was my experience from the beginning. Then and later on I was able to console myself with the thought that I foresaw how it would be. Still, one cannot always anticipate unpleasantness, and it is the unexpected which, as I found, is often the hardest thing to overcome. My situation seemed one which held insurmountable difficulties. This I attri-buted, with some justification, to the shortcomings of my education, and especially to the fact that my univer-sity career had been discontinued.

I meant to be an educator and teacher. As far as I knew, I had to do this freely and independently in such a way as, I was just beginning to realise, might meet the needs of man's character and relationships. Every-one finds it difficult to understand himself, and I found it particularly so; I began to think that I must look for help outside myself and try to gain from others the knowledge and skill I needed.

So I thought again of preparing myself to direct an educational enterprise of my own by continuing my university training, but there was the fact that I had withdrawn from this particular path. As soon as I felt my inadequacy, I not only looked for the remedy in Nature, which fate had determined should be my school, but also turned to the men who had divided the field of education into separate areas of knowledge and had provided us with a vast literature.

I was so depressed and worried by this need for help that I intended to give up my educational work and try to go again to one of the universities as soon as possible, but I came to see that I had not understood myself and decided to stay where I was. This decision was for me the beginning of great activity in the field of education. My first absorbing idea was the clear conviction that in order to educate properly one must share the life of one's pupil. Then came the question: What is elementary education? What is the value of the methods advocated by Pestalozzi? Above all, what is the purpose of education?

In answering the question 'What is the purpose of education?' I started at that time from the observation that man lives in a world of objects which influence him and which he wishes to influence, and so he must know these objects in their characteristics, their essence and their relation to one another and to mankind.

Objects have form, size and number, and these must be taught.

In talking of the external world I meant only Nature. I lived so in Nature that works of art and of man's labour were nothing to me. So for a long time I found it an effort to agree with Pestalozzi's pupils, Tobler and Hopf, and regard the products of man's labour as an object of elementary education. My point of view was greatly extended when I was able to think of the external world as inclusive of the works of man.

At the level of thought which I had then reached I tried to explain everything through man and his relationship to himself and the outer world. The most significant phrase which occurred to me at that time was—'It is all a unity; everything is based on unity, strives towards and comes back to unity.' It is this striving for unity which is the cause of all the different aspects of human life. But there was a great gap between seeing this truth in my own mind and being able to understand and act on it.

It seemed to me that everything which can and should be done through education is, in the nature of the stages of development through which he must pass, implied and given in man and in the relationships in which he is set, and the educated man is one who has been brought up to respect and recognise these relationships, to see them as a whole and to control them.

During this period I did a great deal of hard work, but I found the methods and purposes of education to be so incoherent and fragmented, so entirely unorganised, that for some years my effort to rationalise them did not get very far. I hoped to know everything in its living or inner relationship, and to show how this happens. Fortunately for me, certain works on education by Seiler,[1] Jean Paul[2] and others came out at this time, which encouraged and stimulated me because I found I agreed with some of their views but not with others.

I knew the Pestalozzian method in its essential characteristics, but I did not see it as a living force such as would meet man's needs. I was oppressed by the fact that there was no organic connection between the subjects of instruction; I certainly felt this strongly although it was not apparent to my pupils.

Free and joyful activity flows from the vision of the whole world as a unity; all life and activity are one, for it is conditional on the essential character of the uni-

[1] Georg Friedrich Seiler (1733–1807), a clergyman in Coburg, wrote on religious and moral themes, e.g. *A Bible for Teachers*.

[2] Jean Paul Friedrich Richter (1763–1825) wrote the educational treatise *Levana, or the Doctrine of Education* in 1807. His statements on the significance of play in the education of young children greatly influenced Froebel.

verse. This, I soon felt convinced, was true education, and so my beginning as an educator was merely my own life and the force of my actions; more than this I was not at all in a position to give.

Why is it that man has so little regard for the advantages he possesses from the very beginning? When I now try to explain the life and work of an educator, instances from that period come freshly into my mind. I look now at that childhood of my life as a teacher and learn from it, just as I look back at the childhood of my life as a man and learn from that too. Why is it that all childhood is unaware of its great riches, which are lost before they can be appreciated? Must this always be so? Must it be so for every child? Surely there will soon come a time when childhood will be protected by the experience and insight which age and wisdom bring? What is the use to mankind of the old man's wisdom and experience if he takes them with him into the grave?

My life and work with my pupils was at first very limited, for it consisted merely in living, going out and walking in the open air. As yet I did not bring the simple life of Nature within the sphere of education—it was my pupils who taught me that. In view of my own educational background I encouraged every sign of a feeling for Nature, and so they soon experienced that enjoyment of natural objects which enriches and enhances our lives...

It is intended that man should recognise Nature in her multiplicity of form and shape, and also that he should understand her modes of being and come to a realisation of her unity. So in his own development he follows the course of Nature and imitates her modes of creation in his games. He likes to build and to imitate the structuring of form which we find in Nature's first activity, in the formation of crystals.

However, it must be sufficient now merely to indicate that there is a deeper meaning beneath children's games and occupations. This process of self-employment has not yet been studied at any depth or considered in what might be called its cosmic and anthropological significance. So at any moment, I expect, someone will write a book about it. As I see the loving attention and pleasure with which children work at these occupations another important point occurs to me.

Play necessarily connects the boy with a wider world. If he is building a house, he builds it so that he can live in it as grown-up people do, so that he can have his own cupboard and so on, and be able to give them something out of it. One should be careful not to give a child the sort of gift which will overwhelm him, for it is important that he should be able to give something in return. In fact, it is necessary for him to do so, and he is happy when he knows how to meet this need by making various things which he can give away.

The child has the human need to please and to give. He feels already that he is a part of the whole world and belongs to the whole of Nature, and he wants to be recognised and treated as such. When this happens, the most important means of development open to a human being at this stage has been discovered. The good-natured child values only that which can serve as a shared possession, a bond of union between himself and those he loves. This should be noticed by parents and teachers and used to arouse and develop his impulse to activity and expression. No gift, however small, which a child makes should ever be disregarded.

To comment briefly on my first attempt as an educator, I tried in all earnestness to give my pupils the best possible instruction and training, but my position at that time and my own level of education made it impossible for me to succeed.

2 Letter to Karl Christoph Friedrich Krause (1828)

W. Lange, *Friedrich Fröbels gesammelte pädagogische Schriften*, vol. I, pt. I, pp. 134–43

... After the war of the spring of 1813 had interrupted my studies I returned to Berlin in 1814 to resume them and take up a scientific post. My work was to classify and partly to research into crystals. I worked under Weiss as an assistant at the mineralogical museum of the university. I had then attained my aim; for me now theory and its application, life, Nature and mathematics were all to be studied in a single formation, the crystal, and a world of symbols opened before me.

It had long been my dearest wish to devote myself to an academic career, for I thought to find in it my vocation, the meaning of my life. But the opportunity to get to know students and see their slight knowledge of the subject, their small feeling for it, and still more their lack of any true scientific spirit made me go back on my purpose. I became all the more strongly aware of man's claims to a life which should express his essential being, and so I began to think earnestly again about education and teaching. Therefore I stayed in my post only for two years, but meanwhile the stones in my hand and under my eyes became forms of life which spoke a language I understood. The world of crystals clearly proclaimed the structure of man's life to me and spoke of the real life of his world.

I gave up everything and went back to education. I had to go back and try to apply to the education of man those laws of the development of being which I had glimpsed and seen reflected in Nature. I had to educate man in accordance with the law of development to a realisation of his essential nature. So I gave up my position and left Berlin. Late in the autumn of 1816 I founded the educational work which, though it still exists under my influence and guidance, in the highest degree stands on its own.

I founded it by myself without any material resources at all, trusting in the eternal truth on which it was based and in God who has let the whole ideal flower in my heart—he who let me look into his world and gave me energy and courage to risk all for its realisation. I conceived this work—even if I could not put it into words —as of cosmic scope and lasting importance for mankind. Yet I connected it for this very reason with my own personal life. Since I had no family of my own I associated my enterprise with my beloved nephews and with my native land of Schwarzburg and Thuringia and so with my real fatherland.

I was very diffident about using the words 'German' or 'Universal German' in the title and, indeed, struck them out of one of the manuscripts, yet they exactly expressed the original intention and nature of the institution. I thought that an appeal to the public to be men would be too grandiose and in all likelihood would be misunderstood, as proved to be only too true. If they were asked only to become Germans they would, so I thought, take this seriously and think it worthwhile, especially after the painful experiences they had just suffered.

Justifiably you found fault with this term. Yet even

the appeal to become German was too much, for everyone said, 'I am German, have been German from birth.
Surely that is something I do not have to be taught?'
What would they have said if I'd talked of teaching
them to be men? But if on the contrary I had an-
nounced that I would educate them specifically to be
servants, shoemakers or tailors, merchants or business
men, soldiers or even noblemen, then I should certainly
have won praise for the usefulness of my institution,
and everybody would have looked on it as something
deserving adequate support from the State. I should
have become a State-machine; I should have been busy
cutting out and shaping other machines. But I wanted
to educate men to be free, to think, to take action for
themselves.

Who wants to be any of these things or wants them
for his children? If it was foolish to educate Germans,
how much more foolish would it have been to educate
men. The first was regarded as too difficult, the second
as an illusion.

From this digression I return to the attempt to
explain myself to you, as far as I can do so in a letter,
by setting out my hopes and my endeavours. Let me,
then, go further and try to communicate my deepest
thoughts.

I chose first of all to explain my search for knowledge;
now let me refer to my other aim. My experiences,
especially those of my university career, had taught me
quite unequivocally that existing educational methods,
especially if mere instruction or the communication of
external facts and historical explanations was the aim,
blunted—I might even say destroyed—any attempt in
the schools to promote true knowledge or give any
genuine scientific training. It was my firm conviction,

which I still hold, that the entire system of instruction, even that part of it which had been improved, should be radically revised and the emphasis placed on creation and growth. What I really wanted was the complete antithesis of everything then done in the way of education and instruction.

I felt bound to take this up in a practical way and start it in actual fact. Our greatest teachers, even Pestalozzi, seemed to me too crudely empirical. In my view they were not scientific enough, i.e. they would not be guided by essential reality and its principles, and they failed to recognise or value science in its divine nature.

In my inexperience I thought that my efforts would be acknowledged and supported by the learned world. But in this I was mistaken. Your article in the *Isis* was the only ray of light I saw. The universities took no notice and the reviewers would not accept my views; but my convictions were never shaken, so why should I take any more notice of their denigrating remarks?

I consider that there is a universal pattern of development. When a certain level has been reached after a period of growth, there is a point of culmination. At this stage and in the form it has now reached everything passes through an exactly opposite cycle so that with a clearer, more intense knowledge of itself it comes back to the unity of being. Having assimilated this experience, it then goes forward with energy restored and life renewed for a still higher level of growth. To put it more briefly, I regard the simple pattern of development from the analytical to the synthetical, such as I find in pure thought, as the course of development of all being.

I see mankind about to start on a new course and

enter another age. A new world is beginning, creating an altogether new life for science, initiating the true science, i.e. the science of being, with all that it implies. I believe that the establishment of a school of development which meets these needs would enable our universities to become places where the highest truths are perceived and expressed. My work and the purpose of my educational institute in relation to higher education may be symbolised in the life of the family. It is the mother who first cares for the child and teaches him to be observant and attentive. In her teaching she starts from and refers to the essential unity of all things. When the boy is handed over to his father, his mind is already stimulated with the desire to know cause and effect and to understand life in its entirety and its detail. His mind and eyes are open; he has been constantly encouraged in his desire for activity; he is able to create, observe and analyse; he is active, thoughtful, creative and purposeful. The father takes over such a boy from the mother to instruct him for the wider life outside the home. In this image my educational work is like that of the mother who quietly influences and carefully fosters her children.

All existence and therefore all observation and knowledge begin in action. True education must originate in activity and must similarly be both instructive and creative and must provide for climax and consolidation in the creative process. Living, doing, knowing—these are coincidental, however different the emphasis may be at any one time. If they are completely separated they lead to that 'struggling with life and with death, hanging between them both' which we see so often. There is no creative process unless one's knowledge and insight are advanced and one's life intensified;

there is no move forward into knowledge unless one thinks back and preserves what is already known; there is no active life unless there is also relaxation.

Man should not be satisfied with an education which meets his needs only as a creature of this world but must be thoroughly prepared for all the phases of development in the natural world with which he is confronted, for the eternal here and beyond of each new moment of life, for eternal activity and life in God.

3   *Letter to the women in Keilhau* (*1831*)

Brief an die Frauen in Keilhau, pp. 113–14, 135–6, 137–8, 138–40

...I should have recognised the fact that my life, and indeed all life, shows a certain pattern, and that every move forward after a period of conservation and restraint is strong and vigorous. Above all, I should have already remarked in my life a fact which I just now indicated when referring to the end of my stay in Berlin, and realised its significance for the future, namely that for me a period of quiet fulfilment is followed by one of excitement and investigation when all that I have gained recedes as if behind a veil. I see now at last the inescapable and absolute requirement of my view of life and my vocation. I only value a life which is clearly conscious of itself and term this at its highest level truly human life. I recognise it as my vocation that I have to find life's absolute laws and explain them clearly and so raise man's life to consciousness of itself in its direction, means and purpose.

The art of living is as difficult as any other and no less conditioned and conformable to law. But I believe that mankind does not yet possess this art, not even the starting point. It is my vocation to give mankind this

44

starting point; it is my purpose to find and infer the absolute principles of life from the development of Nature. This has never been taught as a system of vital knowledge or in its use and application as a growing and comprehensive science, at least not as a possession of all mankind...

As you know, the number three is for me a symbol of an absolute, undivided whole, a symbol of fidelity. Also every circle is for me full of symbolic significance. The ball or sphere is a symbol of perfection, of something complete and finished; it is the symbol of my fundamental spherical principles of education and life. This is the explanation of the Keilhau seal of three intertwined circles arranged triangularly and surrounded by twelve stars, which signifies that the educational principles of this institution are in their deepest meaning valid for all...

The mind essentially strives to make evident to itself in visible shape and form all the ideas that live enclosed within it. It may be thought that if the formative power of the spirit—the perceptive power of the mind, one might say—had been brought to a high level, its fundamental mode of thought and feeling would have found in the world confronting it an appropriate form, and would, as it were, have assumed it—such a form as a flower, a stone or any other sort of symbol. However this may be and however many other possible forms it may assume, there is a pattern of thought, perception and feeling which is completely contained in these symbols. For this we should be thankful, since countless significant thoughts, perceptions and feelings ebb and flow in man, which he neither notices nor even suspects because there are no material means for their expression, and which he fails to develop fully in the sense of revealing them in every possible material form. Whatever the cause of substance and form, we have reason to be grateful to it for the ease with which they express our ideas. This points, however distantly and unconsciously, to a definite affinity of mind, intuition, heart and soul. This is important, since nothing at all is more significant for the advancement of man than that he should be convinced of this affinity, for from it springs spiritual life, life in its highest meaning...

But I have not finished my explanation of the ring. A fundamental condition for the attainment of its purpose by every living thing is that it should be faithful to its own life in thought and deed and in every phase of its development. Success is achieved if one is faithful to life, observing and examining it in its individual and general reference. This is a conviction which grows in a man as his own particular life develops. This, I consider, is one of the first concerns of education. It is my belief, a belief which I have held since 1816 and which my time in Griesheim and Keilhau only endorsed, that the more I followed the faint intuitions of what my life needed for its growth the more positive and eventually fruitful they became. The loss of this intuitiveness which I had in youth has often grieved me; I know that man's nature and purpose require that he should not live alone but develop in a social context, yet I realise that this robs life of its clarity and certainty. It has therefore long been one of my endeavours to regain that inward peace, but it seemed impossible because, as I retreated from personal relations, I lost the means of achieving an all-inclusive effect. Yet if my life's work were to be achieved, if even a beginning were to be made, it would be found above all in my constant affirmation of the fundamental concept of life as I saw it. I could realise my earlier vision only if I retained the conviction that man's nature is essentially and innately spiritual. I saw this expressed through the concept of God as creator— therefore the world had a sure existence and basis of development. I saw it expressed in the life and work of Jesus and in the workings of the Holy Spirit.

So I saw in the ring confirmation and expression of my own convictions and came to cherish it as full of meaning for me personally. It seems to me that man's dual nature as body and mind, and above all his essential creativity, lead him to create visible expressions of his mind's activity, to see himself symbolically, as it were. I believe that man is deprived of one of the principal means of self-education and self-knowledge if one takes from him that power to create symbols, to see ideas given visible form. It is very foolish to object to the use of this power on the grounds that a symbol never gives true expression to a concept, for if this were so God would not have created a world which reveals his essential being. It is just as foolish to substitute symbol for idea, for this would be to make Nature, the physical world, equal to God.

It is here my intention only to point out how important the symbol is in the work of education, in the self-education of a rational being. At least it was and still is important for me. I consider it above all else important that it should be applied to the business of education, and I could very easily substantiate this by reference to man's threefold nature as expressed in activity, feeling and thought, or as body, mind and spirit.

Therefore from that time onwards I saw in the ring a symbol of my own fundamental thought and an aid to the recollection of it in every moment of my life, and I am not ashamed to confess that this is really so.

II THE EDUCATION OF MAN:
GENERAL PRINCIPLES

Whenever Froebel was asked where his basic principles were to be found he replied that they were all in the first part of *The Education of Man*. These pages of his greatest work are not a lucid and comprehensive statement of educational theory as such; the writing is characteristically at the level either of profound comment on the universe or of detailed observations on children's behaviour. Yet the fundamentals are here—the belief that we live in a universe which is intelligible only in terms of divine principle: the definition of man's purpose and the educator's function: the subtle analysis of the problems which a real relationship between parent or teacher and the child involves: the emphasis on dynamic growth, on the child's mental activity and total response to his environment from birth and his need to see meaning and purpose in all his activities at all phases of his development.

The Education of Man

E. Hoffmann, *Fröbel. Ausgewählte Schriften*, II, 7–31

An eternal law pervades and rules all things. It is expressed in the external world of Nature, in the inner world of mind and spirit, and in life where these two are unified. It is clearly evident to the person who is convinced by temperament and belief that this must be so, as well as to him who has arrived logically at the view that our minds are revealed in our actions and that our actions are essentially the result of inner realities. Underlying this universal order of things is a living unity which is all-pervading, self-cognisant and everlasting. This unity too is known by faith or perceptive observation, as it has been known at all times by those who respond to it emotionally or who logically apprehend it, and so it will always be.

This unity is God.

Everything has emanated from the divine, from God, and is solely conditioned by God, who is the only cause of all things.

God pervades and rules all things. Everything lives and has its being in and through God. It exists only because God moves within it, and this divine element is its essence.

Everything has a purpose, which is to realise its essence, the divine nature developing within it, and so to reveal God in the transitory world. Man has a special purpose. As a perceptive and rational being, he is intended to reach full awareness of his essential nature. He is meant to reveal the divine element within him by allowing it to become freely effective in his life.

Education, therefore, is the treatment of man as a creature who is developing in awareness and understanding of himself. It should stimulate him to this realisation and show him how to achieve it. Education becomes a science when the educator in and through himself realises and practises the science of life—when he recognises this eternal order of things and understands its cause and its coherence, when he knows life in its totality. Educational theory consists in the principles derived from such insight, which enable intelligent beings to become aware of their calling and achieve the purpose for which they are created. The art of education lies in the free application of this knowledge and insight to the development and training of men, so that they are enabled to achieve their purpose as rational beings. Education, therefore, aims at the realisation of a life which is true to its calling. When such knowledge and practice, such awareness and fulfilment occur in life, then it may be said that wisdom is achieved.

To have such wisdom should be man's highest aim, and to attain it is the highest level of personal achievement. Wisdom is shown when one educates oneself and others in freedom and self-awareness. This process started at the beginning of human history and was established when individual men first began to show full self-awareness; now it is being stated as a universal human demand and as such is beginning to be recognised. It is the only way by which man achieves true happiness, since it leads him to the fulfilment of all that his nature demands.

So education must develop man's essential nature. It must make him consciously accept and freely realise the divine power which activates him. It should lead him to perceive and know the divine as it is manifested in his natural surroundings. It should also, by showing their interrelation, establish the fact that similar laws connect and underlie the world of man and the world of Nature, and bring men to awareness that these worlds proceed from and are conditioned by God and have their being in him. So by education man is to be guided to understand himself, to be at peace with Nature, and to be united with God.

In all these requirements education is grounded on the life of the mind. Yet all such life, as also the divine essence that pervades all things, comes to be known in and through outward manifestation. Therefore education, all life as a creation of freedom, has to do with these outward concerns of man and of things, and through them has its effect on the inner life. This is not, however, a matter of simple inference, for it is in the nature of things that in some relationships inferences cannot be directly drawn. In the relationship between God and Nature the inference must be drawn inversely from the diversity of the physical world to the oneness of God, who is its final ground, and from the oneness of God to unending diversity in the development of Nature. When assumptions about children's attitudes are drawn from their behaviour, then widespread mistakes can be made. Many misconceptions arise and, as a result, parents blame their children or have foolish expectations. If parents and teachers are to establish secure and happy relations with children, then they must try to act on this precept. The child who gives the appearance of being good is often not intrinsically good, that is, does not want what is good of his own choice or out of love and respect for it. The child who seems rude and self-willed is often involved in an intense struggle to realise the good by his own effort. The boy who appears unresponsive may really be steadily intent on a line of thought such as claims his whole attention.

Basically, therefore, education must be permissive and following, guarding and protecting only; it should neither direct nor determine nor interfere.

It must be so, since divine action cannot be other than good if left undisturbed. This implies that the child in his growth positively seeks that which is best for himself—though he may do so unconsciously—in a form appropriate to his abilities and means. In the same way the duckling hurries into the water, the chicken scratches in the earth and the young swallow catches its food on the wing. These conclusions on behaviour and growth, however strongly opposed, will in time be affirmed and their application to education fully vindicated.

To young plants and animals we give space and time, knowing that then they will grow correctly according to inherent law; we give them rest and avoid any violent interference such as disturbs healthy growth. But the human being is regarded as a piece of wax or a lump of clay which can be moulded into any shape we choose. Why is it that we close our minds to the lesson which Nature silently teaches? Wild plants which grow where they are crowded and confined scarcely suggest any shape of their own, but if we see them growing freely in the fields we can then observe their ordered life and form—a sun's shape, a radiant star, springs from the earth. So children who are early forced by their parents into a pattern and purpose unsuited to their nature might have grown in beauty and in the fullness of their powers.

If we take account of divine action and consider man in his original state, it is clear that all teaching which prescribes and determines must impede, destroy, annihilate. To take another example from Nature—the vine has to be pruned, but pruning as such does not bring more wine; however good the intention, the vine may be entirely ruined in the process or its fertility destroyed unless the gardener pays attention to the plant's natural growth. In our treatment of natural objects we often go right, whereas we can get on to an entirely wrong track in dealing with human beings. Yet forces are at work in both which flow from one source and obey the same law—and this is an aspect of Nature which it is important for man to observe.

It is true that we now seldom see the unspoiled original state, especially in human beings. For that very reason it is all the more necessary to assume it until it has been clearly proved that it does not exist. Otherwise there is a danger that, where it is still to be found, it will only too easily be destroyed. However, if the child gives unmistakable evidence that his original state has been entirely vitiated, then methods of control and direction may have to enter in full force into his education. Yet it must be realised that it is difficult to establish proof that an individual's mind has been harmed, and it is particularly difficult to be certain about the origin and course of the injury. The final test of this can be found only within the individual person himself, and this is yet another reason for education being far more permissive than directive; otherwise there is an end of human progress, which consists in man freely expressing the divine spirit in his life.

Where directive methods are necessary they should start with the person beginning to be aware of himself and of his living unity with God. They should follow on an experience of some living relationship, such as that between father and son or disciple and master, which will establish the true state of things in general and in particular terms. Until the cause and direction of disturbance to the pupil's original state have been shown in detail and clearly established, nothing can be done except to bring him into relationships and surroundings where he can be under observation and where his behaviour can be revealed to him, as if it were reflected in a mirror, so that he begins to see its effects and consequences. In this situation his true state can be recognised by himself and others, and the manifestations of his disturbed condition do the least harm.

There are only two arguments that can be advanced

in favour of an education which is directive. These are that it teaches the true self-evident idea or the established and accepted ideal. Yet in reference to the first argument it should be noticed that the self-evident truth, the vital idea, derives its authority from the eternal principle—and this is, therefore, yet another reason for permissive action, since the eternal divine principle itself demands spontaneity and self-determination on the part of human beings who are created for freedom in the image of God. To take the second line of argument, it should be borne in mind that the accepted ideal or the perfect life is intended to serve as a model only in its aim and essence, never in its form. It is a profound misconception to take those human beings who exemplify the spiritual life as formal models, for the usual effect is to check and restrain rather than to uplift mankind. Throughout his life Jesus himself attacked such clinging to an external standard. The ideal should be regarded as an example only in its living aspiration; its form and manifestation should be free. The perfect life which we as Christians see in Jesus was a life which was lived in clear and vivid awareness of the original ground of its being, and which came from the eternal creator self-active and self-reliant. Through the pattern of his life Jesus requires each human being to become such a copy of the eternal ideal and, in his turn, such a pattern for himself and others that he advances freely according to eternal law by his own determination and his own choice. This is the function and purpose of all education, and should be the only one. Therefore, in respect of the form which it requires, the eternal ideal is itself permissive.

Yet this ideal ought to make categorical demands, and it does so. It is, as we see, inexorable and absolute, but only where it is imperatively required by the whole situation and by the nature of the individual and is recognisable as such by the person to whom it is addressed. Here the ideal appears as the agent of necessity, and therefore always speaks conditionally. The ideal acts in this way only when it can be assumed that the person to whom it is addressed either has an intellectual grasp of the reason for the command or accepts it as a matter of faith. Here the ideal does make demands, but only ever in connection with the living spirit and never with mere form.

In true education necessity should call forth freedom, law arouse self-determination, external force develop inner free will, hatred from outside evoke love within. Wherever hatred gives birth to hatred, law to deceit and crime, coercion to slavery, necessity to bondage, wherever oppression destroys and degrades, wherever severity induces obstinacy and falseness, then education has no meaning and no effect. If this is to be avoided, all manifestations of authority should be made with due care and thought. This will happen when all education, which necessarily has the appearance of authority, is throughout characterised by its strict subjection in all its demands to an eternal and inescapable necessity so that there is no sign of capricious and unrestrained power.

The true educator and teacher has to be at every moment and in every demand two-sided. He must give and take, unite and divide, order and follow; he must be active and passive, decisive and permissive, firm and flexible—and so must the pupil. But between teacher and pupil there must rule unseen a third factor—this is the ideal good, the right, which necessarily emerges from the situation and is not an arbitrary expression of power. To this both educator and pupil are subject in exactly equal degree. The educator in particular should give constant and serious expression to his clear understanding and willing acceptance of this dominant factor, for children are able to make fine and accurate distinctions between those requests which are personal and arbitrary and those which are expressions of general imperatives.

Every demand which the teacher makes must in its smallest detail show his submission to this third and changeless element to which both he and his pupil are subject. I would suggest that this should be taken as a general formula for instruction—act and see what follows from your action in a particular situation and to what knowledge it leads you. And for life—show your spiritual being, which is your true life, in and through your actions and see what your nature demands and what it is like. It is in this way that Jesus himself calls upon us to know the divinity of his mission and the truth of his teaching. In this way we attain knowledge of the essential ground of all life and all truth.

This explains the following requirement and at the same time shows how it can be fulfilled. The educator should show the universal aspect of that which is particular and individual and the particular application of that which is generally true. He should make the internal external, the external internal, and show the essential unity of both. He should consider the finite in the light of the infinite and establish an equilibrium in life between them. He should understand and observe the divine in the human, show the essential nature of man in God, and strive to reveal both in their living interrelation. This interrelation is seen all the more surely by man as an essential aspect of his nature the more he observes himself in his own being, in the child and in human history.

Indisputably, therefore, education confronts us with a single aim. It should cultivate man's original divine nature and so it should depict in and through human life that which is infinite and eternal. From the moment of his birth the human being is to be viewed in this light. Possessing an immortal soul, he should be cared for as a manifestation of the divine in human form, as a pledge of God's present love and grace, as a gift of God. Such was the view which the early Christians had of their children, as we can see from the names they gave them. Every child should be accepted as an indispensable and essential member of the human race, and parents should recognise that they are responsible as his guardians to God and to humanity as well as to the child himself. They are required also to consider that the child is in living relationship with the present, past and future of human development, and they should align his education with the challenges of that development. They should treat him as a being with divine, earthly and human attributes who belongs to God, Nature and humanity and who contains within himself present, past and future.

The form of man's life should not be regarded as an immutable fact but as a constant and progressive process of becoming, a continuous advance towards an infinite goal from one stage of growth to another. It is inexpressibly harmful to regard the development and education of man as a static, isolated process which merely repeats itself in different forms. Such a view makes the child merely imitative, an external lifeless copy cast in an earlier mould, and makes it impossible for future generations to see in him a living example of a particular stage of growth in humanity's total development.

Each successive generation and each successive individual should go through the entire pattern of earlier human development—as does in fact happen—otherwise past and present would be incomprehensible. He should do this not by copying and imitating, which is a dead approach, but by the living way of free and independent activity. Every human being should re-interpret this pattern freely, and express human potentiality in an entirely personal and unique manner, so that the nature of man and of God in its infinity and all its diversity becomes ever more exactly discerned.

This full knowledge of a person's nature from the earliest moment is essential and, if seriously pursued, is the source of everything else that needs to be known for his care and education. Parents should realise the worth and dignity of the child as a human being and see themselves as guardians of God's gift. They need to know man's function and destiny and the ways in which he achieves it. The child in his development is intended to reconcile the intellectual quality, which is potentially dominant in his father, with the emotional side of his nature, which is characteristic of his mother. He is also meant, as a child of God and Nature, to realise the harmony between the finite physical world and the infinite world of the divine. As a member of a family, he will reveal its nature and potentiality and show both its unity and its diversity. As a member of the human race, he is called on to develop the powers and abilities of humanity as a whole.

In the membership of a family children fully express the essential character of the group—which may be quite unknown and so far unsuspected by it—if each grows to the full development of all his powers and yet does so in the most deeply individual and personal way. As children of God and members of the human race, men perfectly represent the essential character of God and humanity—which is inherent in them, although not generally recognised or acknowledged—if each one of them in childhood develops as individually and personally as possible. This happens when human development follows the universal pattern and each person realises his nature in the unity of his own being, in the individual character of any particular acts which he initiates, and in the diversity of all he does and influences. Wherever one of these aspects of his nature is not realised or only imperfectly understood, then he fails to achieve full insight into it. It is only if this threefold form of its expression—unity, individuality, diversity—is recognised that the essential character of anything can be completely known.

From birth, therefore, the child should be recognised in his essential nature and allowed to use his energy freely in all its aspects. There should be no hurry to get him to use some of his powers while others are repressed; he should not be bound, confined or swaddled or later on kept in a state of dependence. He should early learn to find in himself the source and centre of all his powers and should move freely and actively, grasp things with his own hands, stand and walk by himself, look and see for himself, and use all his limbs equally and vigorously. He should learn to apply and practise the most difficult of all the arts—to hold fast the focus, the connecting point, of his own life's course when confronted by any impediment.

The child first expresses himself in energetic reactions; he cries, kicks against anything which resists his

59

feet, and grasps whatever his hand touches. Soon after this he develops a feeling for his surroundings; he smiles and shows in his movements his well-being and delight when he is surrounded by comfortable warmth, clear light and fresh air. This in its full development is the beginning of the growth of self-consciousness. So the human being first expresses himself in rest and unrest, pleasure and pain, smiles and tears. As rest, pleasure and smiles indicate whatever a child senses to be appropriate to his untroubled growth, his education in its first beginnings should aim at securing these effects. As unrest, pain and tears indicate whatever adversely affects the child's development, the educator should be concerned to discover and remove their causes. When first the child cries and is restless, he is certainly not behaving badly. But he begins to show the faults of a stubborn and wilful temper when he feels that he has been carelessly abandoned to whatever it is that causes discomfort and pain—and how he feels this and to what degree we cannot tell. When once this feeling has been implanted in his mind he becomes obstinate and self-willed, and then his development may be endangered, for this is a defect which soon engenders other failings and cannot be eradicated without harming some good tendency.

Even when the right way to treat the child's discomfort is adopted, it may be followed incorrectly. Man's development requires that he should be brought up to bear minor afflictions so as to endure more serious hardships. Therefore, once all his needs have been met and anything that can hurt him has been removed, the restless child should be left alone and quietly given time to find himself. If by pretending to be in pain and discomfort the baby has once, let alone repeatedly, secured sympathy, then parents and others have lost ground which they will find it very difficult to regain by compulsion later on. The little creatures have so fine a sense of the weaknesses of those around them that they prefer to use their innate power for the domination of others, which is easier than developing it in themselves by their own patience and effort.

At this stage of his development the human being is called a suckling, and he is so in the fullest sense of the word, for assimilation is almost his only activity. Even the immediate responses of crying and smiling are hardly as yet expressed. He takes in only the diversity of the outer world and absorbs it in himself. His whole being is merely an appropriating eye. Therefore this first phase is incalculably important for his present and future development. Nothing detrimental should be fixed in his mind at this stage. The people around him should treat him in such a way that he feels confident and secure. Unfortunately, throughout his life, man rarely shakes off the impressions absorbed in childhood just because his whole being is opened like a great eye and he is wholly surrendered to them. In later life a person's hardest struggles with himself and his most serious setbacks are often grounded in this phase of his growth, and for this reason the care of the infant child is so important. The child's first smile, as mothers know, marks a very definite period in his life, since it is his first physical discovery of himself. It may be much more than that, for it originates not merely in a physical sensation of a separate self but also in a higher feeling of relationship at first with the mother, then with the father and the family, and later on with other human beings.

The child's first feeling of community with his family

is later connected with his perception that the several members of the family recognise that they are in a relationship of unity with humanity and with God. This sense of community is the first beginning of all true religious feeling, of all genuine striving for unimpeded union with the eternal. If religion is to live and endure, it must come to man in early childhood when the innate divine spirit is yet dimly aware of its origin, and this obscure awareness must be fostered and strengthened in the child so that later in life he may clearly apprehend it.

If parents want to give their children the great gift of this constant and sustaining relationship, they must be united with them whenever in prayer they acknowledge their union with God. It should never be said that children will not understand this unity, for that is to rob them of the highest good. They can certainly understand it if only they have not already become estranged from themselves and their parents, and they do so instinctively, not by abstract reasoning. If a person has not grown up from childhood with deep religious convictions, he will only with the greatest difficulty achieve them later on, but if a sense of religion is implanted in the earliest years by the example of his parents' life—even though he may apparently not understand or even notice it—it will survive.

It is important not only for his religious training but also for his whole education that the child's progress is regarded as a continuous advance. Great harm is done if, within the cycle of the formative years, such sharp divisions and contrasts are made that their sequence and connection, their living core, are forgotten. It is wrong to regard the stages of development—infancy, childhood, youth, maturity, old age—as separate and distinct, since life shows us that they merge into one another. Yet the child is regarded as entirely different from the youth or the adult. They are so far removed from him that their ideas and speech scarcely suggest their common humanity, and the lives they lead give not the slightest hint of it. Even within childhood infancy is distinguished as an entirely separate phase, and in later life people speak of the young as if they were completely alien to them. The boy does not see the child in himself or foresee the growth of a child into boyhood. The adolescent similarly rejects any connection between himself and the boy. Worst of all, the man no longer sees in himself the early stages of his development but speaks of the child or the adolescent as another kind of being of entirely different nature and disposition.

This setting of divisions and sharp limits arises when we fail to give early and sustained attention to our own life—a failing which causes untold harm to human development in general. It requires rare strength of mind in a person to overcome the limits imposed by those who have influence on him. Even if they are overcome, it can only happen through a violent upheaval which may destroy or at least repress other developments. Even so, if this has happened to any person at any stage, then all his actions throughout his life retain something of violence. It would be entirely different if parents were to envisage the child in relation to all stages of human age and growth without exception, and especially if they were to bear in mind that the full development of each successive stage depends on the complete and special development of every single preceding phase. Yet they foolishly ignore this. They look on their child as a boy or an adolescent when he reaches a certain age. Yet he does not reach boyhood or adolescence by being so many years old but by satisfying the intellectual, emotional and physical needs of the preceding phase. Similarly the adult reaches maturity if he has fulfilled the demands of childhood and adolescence. Parents who otherwise seem sensible expect the boy to act like a man. But it is one thing to respect the child's potentiality and quite another to expect him to think and behave as a mature person. When parents make these demands they have overlooked the fact that they themselves have become responsible people only because they have lived through the experiences of each phase of growth. Yet they are now denying these experiences to their children.

The teacher's task later on becomes almost impossibly difficult as a result of this underestimation of the earliest stages of growth. If a boy has been brought up in this way he thinks he can simply ignore all the instruction which has been appropriate to the earlier period. If some extraneous aim such as preparation for a special position or a career is set for him at an early age, then he is put at a disadvantage. At every age a person's only aim should be to fulfil the needs of the particular stage of his existence, and then he will try to meet its special demands. Satisfactory development at any one period can be achieved only if there has been fulfilment at the earlier levels of growth.

It is important to consider this point in relation to productive activity. At present people have an entirely false and degrading idea of work which is done for material results. God himself works continuously to create and to produce. We have only to look at the life and work of Jesus or, if we live true to ourselves, at our own lives and work. The spirit of God hovered over the

64

shapeless void, and stones and plants, animals and men, were formed and given life. So man, who has been made by God in his own likeness, should create shape and form. This is the deep meaning of work, of productive and creative activity. Through our work we become like God if, in doing it, we know or even vaguely feel that we are giving visible form to the spirit that is within us. Insight into the nature of God comes to us in our work. Here the words of Jesus are forever true—the poor do indeed possess the kingdom of heaven if they would only know it and realise it in their daily work. So do children; if unchecked by adult presumption and folly, they will give themselves up to their innate desire for activity and creative work.

The idea that man labours only to get material things and to earn food, shelter and clothing is illusory and degrading. He works primarily to give outward form to the divine spirit within him so that he may know his own nature and the nature of God. In comparison, material returns are an unimportant increment. Jesus says, 'Seek ye first the kingdom of heaven'; so you must work to show in your life that which is divine, and whatever else you need will be added unto you. Jesus also said that his purpose was to do the will of God, to work as and how God commanded. We consider that the lilies of the field do not toil, yet they are sending forth leaves and flowers and in their beauty making known the nature of God. We consider that the birds of the air do not labour, yet they are showing in their singing, in the building of their nests and in all that they do the life which God has given them. So man should learn to reveal in his work, however important or unimportant it seems, the nature God has given him, and he should do this as time and place, status and calling require. If he does so he will be materially secure, for he has his intelligence and can find within himself or in his surroundings a way to satisfy his needs.

All operations of the spirit are manifested in time, in sequence. If a person has at any period of his life failed to express in work the powers which are derived from God, he will find that he cannot make good this omission at any other time. He will find that he has missed the chain of effect which his neglected action would have created, and he can do nothing but accept the situation and try to avoid such a mistake in the future.

It becomes clear that, from earliest childhood, man should be trained in productive activity, since the development of both mind and body demands it. Its first sign is the baby's activity of sense and limb; then it flowers into the child's play as he is busy creating shape and form; and this is the time to implant the seeds of activity and effort for the future. All children and adolescents, whatever their rank or position, ought to spend one or two hours a day on specific, productive work. The lessons to be learnt from daily life and work are by far the most effective and intelligible and have the most vital significance; yet children, and mankind in general, nowadays give far too much attention to uncreative pursuits and too little to real work. Since parents and children have the attitude that work is unimportant and even harmful, it is the function of educational institutions to correct this. At present an untold amount of human energy remains undeveloped because the education given at home or school discourages physical effort and work. It would be beneficial if schools were to introduce proper hours of work in addition to the hours of instruction—indeed, they will have to do it. So far man has used his energies to little purpose and restricted them to the furtherance of material ends and, in consequence, has ceased to value or appreciate them.

Early training for purposeful activity is as important as early training in religion which, indeed, it strengthens if its significance is understood. Religion without purposeful activity risks becoming empty dreaming or futile enthusiasm, just as work without religion makes man a beast of burden, a machine. Work and religion are co-existent. God the eternal is eternally creative.

Yet the human mind should develop its power not only through the inward peace of piety or the outward expression of active work but also from its own resources. This is achieved by self-control and moderation; for those who are not entirely unaware of their own nature it is surely unnecessary to do more than to state this fact. In this union of religion, purposeful activity and self-control all human felicity is to be found.

Thus in the child the human being as a whole is evident, for in childhood the life of humanity appears as a unity. The whole future activity of the man is to be seen germinally in the child. In order that he himself and humanity in him may reach full development, man must from childhood be envisaged as a unity and must be seen in the totality of his earthly relationships. But as all unity requires for its manifestation particular and individual things, and as all universality in its manifestation is conditioned by the sequence of time, so the world and life unfold to the child and are developed in him only in separate and successive experiences. Therefore, the child's powers and aptitudes and his physical and mental activities should be developed in the order of succession in which they emerge in his life.

III THE YOUNG CHILD

In practice Froebel worked from the experiments with children of school age to his great work in the field of the education of the youngest children. Yet his intense interest in this field, which had started in the years with Pestalozzi, was apparent long before it flowered into the special Kindergarten writings. His close observation of young children is to be seen in the detailed notes—*Summary of the story of a child's development during the first period of life*—which exist in an undated manuscript in his own writing; it is likely that this summary was made for the childless Froebel by his closest colleague, Middendorff, when his first son was born about 1830. Already in 1826 Froebel had written with deep perception of the need to observe and interpret such growth in the essay on *The small child, or the importance of a baby's activities*. In *The Education of Man* also there is a considerable section on childhood, where he develops the theme of the child's response to his environment and his growth within the family group.

From his writings in the mid 1830s it is clear that he had reached another critical point in the understanding of his vocation. Now his vision was of the urgent need to provide the pre-school child up to the age of six or seven with the sort of activities and material which his true development demanded. He talked fervently of a renewal of life for mankind. He believed that he had opened up a new world by discovering the meaning of children's behaviour and by devising for them a series of playthings and games. These playthings, which were his 'gifts' to children, were described as he devised them in the *Sunday Journal* which he produced between 1838 and 1840 and which his first editor, Lange, included in the volume translated as *Pedagogics of the Kindergarten*.

The extracts from the *Pedagogics* given here are chosen primarily to show Froebel's reasons for the choice and use of play materials and games rather than their characteristic features. The playthings or 'gifts' formed a sequence: the first was a number of soft balls; the second was a set which comprised a wooden sphere, cube and cylinder; the third, fourth, fifth, and sixth were large cubes divisible into small cubes, oblongs and prisms. In addition to the play series built on the 'gifts' Froebel devised a sequence of 'occupations' which trained children in such activities as drawing, modelling in clay, and using paper and pliable materials in a multiplicity of ways. In themselves the 'gifts' formed an elaborate sequence which, if imposed on children, could become a didactic routine. Froebel justified them by his conviction that they were revealed to him by the children themselves. Certainly his insight into children's behaviour is often a startling illumination, but his interpretation when translated into a pedagogic system, and above all when divorced from his own profound belief in its symbolic meaning, became a chilling formalism.

The institution already started was given its significant name of Kindergarten in 1840 and launched as a new educational venture in a series of appeals. At this stage Froebel summoned women to play a more positive part in education and recognise their own function and dignity. So the first *Outline of a plan* for the Kindergarten began with such an appeal.

In his writings, apart from the numerous appeals for support and the constant working out of his ideas in voluminous letters, the further development of his work in this field was a book for mothers—the *Mutter- und Kose-Lieder*—published in 1843. It contained songs and finger plays for the occupation of mother and child accompanied by pages of complex illustrations, prefatory remarks in rhyme, and long prose explanations of the purpose and symbolic meaning of the activities. It is impossible to make any selection from this book since each game and song, picture and commentary, forms an integral whole. Though it was highly valued by Kindergartners and certainly showed deep insights into the child's growth and also broke new ground as an educational venture, it is a curiosity.

1   *Summary of the story of a child's development during the first period of life*

E. Hoffmann, *Fröbel. Ausgewählte Schriften*, 1, 89–92

The child was born between ten and eleven o'clock on a bright spring morning. The birth occurred normally and quickly. Face down and with arms outstretched to the ground as though afraid of falling, the child was received on to the nurse's lap. Instantly she wiped his mouth and he at once uttered a loud cry. His eyes were open.

When he was washed all his skin appeared red. Then, immediately after the first attentions had been given to him, he was put on the bed where he lay peacefully and quietly, his eyes gazing around; then he was washed with warm water, whereupon he moved restlessly as if it were an unpleasant sensation.

He weighed six pounds and was about nineteen inches long. His body was perfectly formed.

His expression was cheerful, almost as if he were already about to smile, and then it would become serious again.

After he had been washed and then dressed in soft white linen, he was loosely covered up but his arms were left free.

Soon after this, about half an hour after birth, the child fell asleep, presumably tired out by the recent excitement. He had put his hands on to his face and had folded his fingers together; all his fingers were clasped together and his arms arched outwards. They were used to this position in his mother's womb.

If they were touched, his hands always moved first apart and then together again, and sometimes he would suddenly knock them together. If a finger were held out to him, he would at once hold on to it firmly though not for long.

Every physical contact seemed to affect him almost painfully, for his face would screw up, and often a look of tension could be seen in his eyes. So, even on the first day, there was some variation in his facial expressions. In general, however, he looked cheerful.

Four to five hours after birth the child was laid at his mother's breast and he sucked vigorously; as he did so his eyes were open. He did not cry when he was taken away; in general he cried very little. Already in the first days he seemed aware of the purpose of sucking, for he would put his finger to his mouth and open it in order to suck. At this time he moved his head and shoulders restlessly; when put to the breast he made these same movements but with even more violence if he could not get to suck properly. Generally he moved his arms and head a great deal, but he was not imperious in his demands to be fed.

He had resisted the very first washing and at the second, eight hours after birth, he cried and made the same movements as at birth, as though he were frightened of falling.

Already in the first hour of life his eyes adjusted to light, and to a certain extent they turned to look at and linger on any light that was held in front of him. In this reaction the baby showed a sign of that attention which the focusing of the eyes later on reveals. Often he lay there peacefully just gazing around.

Thus already in the first hours of life he revealed free activity.

In the evening and at night he slept peacefully, and on the second day the natural process of excretion occurred.

On the second day all his activities were livelier. He seemed to look into his father's eyes. His right eye was swollen since he had lain with that side facing the light. The second night was just as peaceful as the first.

On the third day he was livelier still and more energetic, but the night was more restless.

On the fourth day he was quieter. When a hyacinth was held in front of his nose it looked as if he wanted to sneeze—so it appears that the olfactory nerve could be stimulated. The night was peaceful.

On the fifth day there was evacuation of the bowels. He was getting adequate nourishment from his feeding. He was obviously healthy since he was thriving and comfortable. Everything was going well.

He looked round at objects such as yellow flowers and green leaves. A blue hyacinth held in front of him seemed to claim his attention, but no more so than any other bright object, yet he gave some indication of the reaction of sneezing. He appeared to be tired by these exertions and yawned several times.

The pupil of the eye had become a little wider and it appeared most enlarged when the baby was feeding. His gaze was calm and attentive and he looked long at objects which attracted him.

This, then, is the first lesson to be drawn, a lesson which the ordinary circumstances of life teach us. A child needs gentle stimulus to develop his visual ability and if this is not provided his mental powers may remain inert. But if the stimulus is prolonged the effect is the same as if it were too strong and the child is overstimulated. True teaching will avoid the two faults of overstimulation and inaction.

On the sixth night the child was rather restless. He now demanded his mother's breast more often.

Every day the child was at his most restless from early evening until midnight, presumably because his energy which had been stimulated by the daylight was then being most strongly expressed.

On the seventh day he was peaceful, looked cheerfully around, noticed many different sorts of objects, even those which were not very bright, and gazed at the faces which were looking at him. When he lay on his stomach, as he did after he had been washed, he was comfortable; then he would lift his head and shoulders backwards. As yet there was no evidence that the power to hear and to smell had been aroused. There were now more varied movements with his hands.

On the eighth day it was noticeable that he gazed directly at an object.

In these first days it had been determined that the child was gifted with a lively disposition and high intelligence.

He had put on one and a half pounds in weight and one and a half inches in height.

From the ninth to the twelfth day as before. He slept much, cried little, worked hard at his feeding but not violently so, was seldom restless but, when he was, he moved his arms vigorously, and was noticeably happy when he was picked up.

Sometimes, after he had been gazing at something for a long time, his eyes seemed to become unfocused, but otherwise he appeared to be gaining more control over them.

In sleep he moved his mouth as if he were sucking; a vague beginning of dreaming; consequently the representations of his though tin action when he was awake were already strongly pronounced.

Until the fourteenth day he showed clearly that he was pleased when he was picked up, for he was quiet when he was laid on his mother's or his sister's lap. He liked best of all to lie on his stomach. All this was already obvious in the first eight days. Now he was sometimes left to lie and cry when it was assumed that he was not in any real need, and he was soon quiet again.

At such times he clearly showed his annoyance by his expression, but on the other hand there were occasions when his expression was one of happiness whenever people looked at him or spoke to him in a friendly way.

2 The small child, or the importance of a baby's activities

E. Hoffmann, *Fröbel. Ausgewählte Schriften*, 1, 79–86

'Unto us a child is born.' 'God has given children to these parents.' 'He has blessed this marriage with children.' What do all these expressions really mean? What in reality is the birth of a child? An invisible spiritual being which has an eternal existence makes its appearance. The invisible becomes visible; that which is infinite, spiritual, divine is manifested as finite, physical, human. Being comes into existence. It is in man's nature that he is essentially eternal, spiritual, divine, existent, and he can be nothing else. Therefore his birth is awaited with hope and joy, for his parents are filled with the idea that an eternal being is coming into finite existence. It is like the dawn of a morning which promises a clear, sunny day. The joy which pervades the whole family is based on the feeling that once again a phenomenon which begins to reveal the high nature of man has entered into existence.

It is the mother in particular who is aware of this in the child, as it is woman's special care to foster the human race in its perpetual renewal. So the German poet calls women to their task of taking thought and educating our posterity for happiness since only they can do it.[1]

The feeling with which the child is first welcomed should surround him always and should lead to careful observation of the way in which he develops and expresses his thoughts. So Mary from the beginning related everything to the higher spiritual life which was to come into existence through her, and so it is said of her that she kept all these things and pondered them in her heart. Yet most people regard the child's behaviour as meaningless in any spiritual sense, and even as merely fortuitous or conditioned only by physical circumstances in the earliest days. This is their view of such an event as the first smile, which instantly distinguishes the young human being from any other creature. It shows that the child has reached the stage where he is becoming conscious and aware of himself. It is an essentially human characteristic, and certainly not a mere expression of physical well-being. It is the way in which the child, while as yet without any means of expression, first enters into communication with other minds. The first smile is, therefore, the expression of an independent human mind which is at the very least developing to consciousness. In this way the child

[1] A reference to the final lines of Herder's poem *Ariadne auf Naxos*.

expresses his ability to make himself understood by another human being and shows that he himself understands. His smile already expresses his personality, his uniqueness (his individuality), yet it is generally disregarded.

Just as little regard is paid to the other significant expressions of the child's life, yet they merit attention. When older brothers and sisters are busily playing with him he is aroused to vigorous activity; the tension in his face and the trembling of his limbs show how much his spirit is striving to get knowledge and control. This, it must be realised, is the expression of a mind trying to overcome the limits put upon it.

How hard the baby tries to respond as his mother lovingly talks away to him! Consider the effort and interest with which he makes sounds—and this is no mere playing with the organs of speech. Notice how he takes up a word, and how he responds to the different tones and expressions of her voice. In himself the child seems to understand or at least to sense that it is to him his mother is speaking and seems in his own way to be answering her, even though he is not yet able to say what is in his mind. It is noticeable that the more the mother's talk touches the child's consciousness the more intensely is this inner life aroused, though it is still limited in its means of expression. In his soul the child wants to break the barriers put up against him and he is impatient at this inability to communicate. Adults who remember something of their own childhood can surely call to mind such feelings of anxiety and should regard this aspect of childhood as the striving of the human spirit to achieve freedom and independence.

No less important is the peculiar intensity with which

very small children focus their eyes on objects which are new or strange to them, especially if they are shining or coloured objects. Notice how much questioning, examining, weighing and comparing is expressed in the child's gaze. Yet this is not the effect of an impression of something strange and unknown, but rather a sign of intense mental activity, of the mind's effort to release itself.

This activity is shown even more clearly in the child's play as he twists and turns, touches things, takes them up and puts them down, and piles up and pushes over anything that is at hand. He is intensely active and continuously occupied, and he is hurt if his plaything is taken away too soon. It is good for a child to concentrate on an object, on a series of mental pictures, for he often needs to be occupied for a long time with some quite simple thing. So we ought not to distract his attention or try to take an object away from him or regard him as destructive if he soon throws everything away. From these and all other manifestations of impulses and actions we should always—in the case of usually healthy children—try to find out the essential motives and reasons and give attention to the mind's activity as it is made known, which means that we should provide children with the most expedient means for the development and strengthening of their minds.

There is within the child a need to attain to consciousness, an urge to find sensory proof of a self-existence of which he is as yet unaware. In earliest childhood this striving towards consciousness can well be more powerful than in many older people. We who are adult in our awareness cannot imagine how intrinsically powerful is this urge in the earliest years. Look at a child whose development is undisturbed and unrestricted and it becomes clear enough. When we are aware of this we must take care to foster it. But how? To the child the sight of the grown-ups around him—and this is very true of his parents who at first command his whole field of vision—is the sun which draws him out; and when he establishes other relationships within and beyond himself, these are the climatic conditions, the broad sky, under which he grows up. To all these impressions and conditions he is more sensitive than the tenderest plant. There lives and acts in the child a soul given by God, a sensitive, highly impressionable, dynamic embodiment of mind and spirit. This must be our real concern from the very moment of the child's birth.

Could we but regard our children in the first weeks of their life as inherently sensitive and responsive to their environment, how different they and how different mankind would be! We must escape the delusion that insight is denied to the child and that he lacks judgement. True, he wants the adult's power of deductive thought, yet he has a certain spontaneous insight and judgement, an immediate response, which is for that very reason all the more likely to be right. With the smallest child, therefore, we should take particular care to search in his mind for the reality from which all this springs. A baby may appear helpless but his power of thought is much greater than we imagine. It is important both for his sake and for our own that all this activity of mind should be observed and remembered. It is important for him because his thoughts are not expressed at the level of consciousness and he can only sense and feel the conditions which give rise to them. For us it is important because we are thereby enabled to extend our insight into that part of our life which is its centre-point.

It is difficult for an observer to pronounce with any truth or certainty on the situations which produce and condition a child's behaviour. Therefore a man needs to have the particular details of his remarks and conduct during childhood preserved so that later on he can analyse his experiences and find in himself traces of the causes of early childhood behaviour. Then gradually he may arrive at full understanding of himself and see his life as an integrated whole. As persons who have ourselves attained self-consciousness in some degree, we must do this for our children if we wish to treat them as beings who are becoming self-aware.

Observation of children is just as important for us too. In doing so we catch sight of our own far-off childhood which, like our own faces, we can see only in a mirror. Through our observation we come to understand ourselves and our own life, which then becomes for us an unbroken whole.

So the family is the place where understanding of the higher values of life is fostered in such a way that cognition and action are never isolated from each other but are always in close association. In the family children are regarded as an enrichment—any other view can be attributed only to self-seeking or lack of thought. In this respect also the devoted care which parents and others give to the helpless child will be rewarding.

Since the behaviour of even the youngest child is of great significance and the expression of his thoughts may so easily be forgotten or confused, parents ought to keep a record of the child's life in which they note down the first signs of his mode of thought, describe and interpret his development in all its aspects, and set down the effects and changes produced in his life and behaviour by certain impressions, situations and ideas.

Such a record would have a dual purpose. It would enlighten parents increasingly about their children, since they could explain their development in the light of earlier happenings and treat them in ways appropriate to their individual dispositions and character. Also children would discover later on that their parents had had a care for their unique personal life, their emotions and thoughts. Undoubtedly one of the mainsprings of a child's behaviour in all his searching and striving is the sort of care bestowed on his particular needs. He soon feels when his own individual self is the object of his parents' care and so comes to have confidence in them. Sensing the living purpose which unites him to them, he grows in love and trust for them and so a genuine relationship develops. The child does not have to experience the frustration of realising that his parents pay no regard to his own subjective life, of whose existence and needs he is himself so intensely aware. He does not have to see his dearest purposes misunderstood and thwarted. And parents are not so often disappointed in their children but come to see that, if only their own ideals and standards are high, their children's life in all its apparent difference is not as remote and alien from their own as they imagine.

'You'll never learn this anyway.' 'You'll never manage to do this.' 'Why do you take on something which you can't possibly do?' Parents and others should not speak so lightly and carelessly to the child and curb the flow of his strength and courage. They should not, on the other hand, expect so much from him as seriously to undermine his power in other ways. On the contrary, if the child is not yet able to achieve something, they will speak encouraging words—'If you work hard and persevere, it will make up for what you lack in natural ability.' Or, in another case, they will give a warning— 'If you are careless and don't pay attention, then you may easily fail to benefit from the gifts you've got.'...

3 The Education of Man: in childhood

E. Hoffmann, *Fröbel. Ausgewählte Schriften*, II, 31, 32, 33–7, 39–40, 41, 44–6, 51–6

To the child the world first appears out of nothingness. It is a vague, shapeless darkness, a chaotic confusion, into which he himself merges. In this nothingness objects begin to be distinguished as his mother and others talk to him. At first their words reveal the outer world as distinct and then as associated with him. Words come singly and slowly in the beginning, then with greater differentiation and frequency, until the child sees himself as a distinct and unique object...

Man's function may be defined in general terms as the giving of outward expression to his inner life, the assimilation of the outer world into his consciousness, and the discovery of their unity. Every object challenges the human being to recognise it in its nature and its relationships. So he has his senses, the tools with which he meets this challenge and assimilates the world outside him...

In the earliest stage of growth the human being is concerned only with the use and exercise of his body, senses and limbs. He is not at all interested in, or indeed aware of, the effects produced by such activity. He makes play with his hands, fingers, lips, tongue and feet as well as with his eyes and facial expressions. This sort of play is not an attempt to give expression to his

6 81

thoughts and feelings; that occurs at the next stage of growth...

The stage of infancy passes into that of childhood when the baby is able to use his physical and sensory activity to show his thoughts and feelings. Up to this stage his mind is merged in an undifferentiated whole of being. As speech develops, however, the child starts to express and organise the life of his mind and to distinguish its manifestations and purposes. It is a characteristic of this period that he strives to express his ideas in tangible shape and form.

With this tendency the education of man properly begins, and there is now less attention to physical growth and more concern for mental development. This phase is the concern of his parents and family with whom he is still most closely associated. As yet the medium of language has no special significance for him; he regards it as a part of himself like his arm, his eye or his tongue.

Yet there is no hierarchy in the stages of human development, apart from the necessary order of their appearance which always makes the earlier the more important. Each is equally important in its own place and time. The great significance of childhood is that it is the period when the child develops his first connections with his environment and makes his first approach to an intelligible interpretation and grasp of its real nature. In his growth it is important to man whether he regards the outer world as meaningless and evil—to be exploited or to be enjoyed only by others—or as intrinsically purposeful and possessed of a high and spiritual function. It matters to him whether it is ennobling or degrading, whether the material relationships which he experiences are true or false. Therefore his surroundings should be correctly and intelligibly presented to the child, and he should be enabled to observe and identify objects in their nature and properties, in their relationships in time and space and in their inter-connections.

It is a characteristic of this period that the child cannot separate the word which he speaks from the object which it describes—word and object are as yet undifferentiated. This is particularly noticeable in his play. While he is playing the child likes to talk; play and speech are the elements in which he now lives. So he invests everything with life and with the faculties of speaking, feeling and hearing. Just because he is beginning to give expression to his own thoughts he assumes that the same activity is occurring in everything around him, whether it is a stone or piece of wood, a plant, a flower or an animal.

So at this stage the child progresses in his own inner life, in his membership of a family where he participates in a relationship with a higher invisible being, and in his life with Nature which he endows with sentient life similar to his own. Throughout childhood he should be allowed to maintain this connection with Nature and its phenomena as a focus of his life, and this is done mainly through the encouragement of his play which at first is only natural life.

Play is the highest level of child development. It is the spontaneous expression of thought and feeling—an expression which his inner life requires. This is the meaning of the word 'play'. It is the purest creation of the child's mind as it is also a pattern and copy of the natural life hidden in man and in all things. So it promotes enjoyment, satisfaction, serenity, and constitutes the source of all that can benefit the child. A child who plays well of his own accord, quietly persisting until he is physically tired out, will develop as an efficient and determined person, ever ready to make sacrifices for the good of himself and others. This age has no lovelier sight than that of a child absorbed in play, so completely absorbed that eventually he falls asleep as he plays.

At this age play is never trivial; it is serious and deeply significant. It needs to be cherished and encouraged by the parents, for in his free choice of play a child reveals the future life of his mind to anyone who has insight into human nature. The forms of play at this age are the core of the whole future, since in them the entire person is developed and revealed in the most sensitive qualities of his mind. A person's life to its very end has its sources in this period when it is determined whether it shall be rich or poor in achievement, and whether he will be gentle or violent, show apathy or intelligent insight, create or destroy. His connections with family and society, with Nature and God, all depend on his mode of life at this time when these relationships are in complete unity. So it is that he scarcely knows which he likes best—the flowers, his own delight in them, his parents' pleasure when he presents them, or his vague intuition of God who gave them. It is impossible to analyse all the joys in which this period is so rich. If a child's development is harmfully affected now, if the core of his future life is impaired, then it will be only with the greatest effort that he will escape permanent injury or at best the restricted growth of his personality.

The aim and object of parental care in the home and family is to stimulate the child's entire powers and natural gifts and enable him to develop them to the full. A mother does this naturally and spontaneously

84

without any instruction or prompting, but this is not enough. It is also necessary that she should influence the child's growing awareness and consciously promote the continuity of his development, and that she should do this by establishing a positive and living relationship with him. So it is our concern to arouse intelligent parental love and show the modes in which childhood expresses itself.

The mother in all simplicity strives to develop the child's full activity of sense and limbs. Unfortunately most of us are too clever to see that this is the starting point of all human development. Having lost the right direction, we are helpless; rejecting God and Nature, we look to human ingenuity. So we build a house of cards in which Nature finds no place and divine influence no room; it falls to the ground at the slightest touch of the child's real desires and impulses, but if it stands he is fettered in mind and body...

The true mother gently follows the life that stirs in the child and so awakens the fuller awareness slumbering in his mind.

Later on the child in his quiet diligence tells us that he must know the properties and uses of all the things he finds, but we dismiss his activity as childish because we fail to understand it or to see, hear and feel as the child does. So to us his life is dead. We cannot explain his activity to ourselves or to him; yet it is longing for explanation which drives him to seek our help. How can we give a language to the objects of the child's life when they do not speak to us? This is what he wants when he brings us something he has found or holds it in his hand as if it could tell him about itself. The child loves everything which enters his range of vision and extends his narrow world. To him the smallest thing is a discovery, but it should have life and meaning for him; otherwise it only obscures his vision. He wants to know why he finds pleasure in an object and what its nature and all its properties are so that one day he will come to understand himself and his likings. So he twists and turns it around, picks it to pieces or puts it in his mouth and tries to bite it. We shout at him and say he is clumsy, but he is much wiser than we are. He needs to know what the object is really like because he is driven by an innate urge which, rightly understood and directed, seeks for a knowledge of God in all his works. For this purpose he has been given reason, understanding and speech. Since the people around him cannot satisfy his need, where else can he look except to the object itself?

The broken object, the stone or the flower can at least show the character of its component parts, and surely this is an extension of knowledge? Does anyone increase his knowledge in any other way? The purpose of the child's activity is to discover from its various aspects the real nature of an object and its relation to himself, and so to establish its attraction for him. Such activity has value and meaning for us if the teacher at his desk does it, but we fail to appreciate it in the child's actions. This is why our children are so often uninfluenced by the most experienced teacher, because they are being obliged to learn things we should have taught them in early childhood when with any encouragement they could have discovered them almost for themselves.

The child requires very little to be given to him; we need only put into words what he is doing and discovering. The life of the growing child is rich but we do not see it, full of vitality but we do not realise it, adequate to the challenges of man's destiny but of this we have no intimation. We not only fail to cherish and develop it but we let it be crushed by the burden of its own efforts or assert itself in artificiality. When we see energies and aptitudes misdirected, like morbid outgrowths of a plant, we want to direct them elsewhere, but it is then too late, for we have not only failed to recognise the significance of the child's life but have also disturbed and repressed its development.

Look, a child has just found a small stone, perhaps a piece of limestone or chalk. He rubs it on a bit of board near at hand and discovers that it makes coloured marks. Delighted with this discovery, he quickly makes use of it and soon covers almost the whole surface of the board. At first it is the fact of discovery which pleases him, then the different colours which appear on the board, but soon his delight is in the shapes he is making. From this his attention turns to the outlines of objects around him; now a head becomes a circle, an oval shape joined on to it is the body, straight or crooked lines are arms or legs, straight lines meeting in a point are fingers, dots are eyes. A new world of ideas and objects opens before him, for one begins to understand that which one strives to represent...

We find a freshness and richness in the life of the child who has been rightly guided and cared for in his early years. Is there any part of a person's thought and feeling, knowledge and ability, which does not have its deepest roots in childhood, any aspect of his future education which does not originate there? To the child the worlds of language and Nature lie open. He is beginning to discover the properties of form, number and size and to have knowledge of space and natural forces and the reactions of different substances. He is starting to understand colour and rhythm, sound and shape. When he is confronted by the outer world as something separate from himself he begins to differentiate the realms of Nature and human skill. And by this time the sense of an inner world of his own has developed within him. So far, however, there is one aspect of his life which we have not mentioned, namely his association with mother and father, sisters and brothers in their daily work.

I look out of doors, and the carter's child, hardly two years old, is leading his father's horse by the bridle. He walks confidently in front and looks firmly round to see that the horse is following. Though his father holds the reins in his hands, the child is quite convinced that he is the one who is leading the horse. When the father stops to speak to an acquaintance, the horse stops also, but the child thinks that the horse is being obstinate and pulls on the bridle with all his strength.

My neighbour's son, scarcely three years old, is minding his mother's goslings near my garden fence. He has to keep the lively little creatures looking for food in a small area, but they escape from him into the road. The mother sees the danger and calls to her son to be careful. The small son, who must often have been put out in his own pursuits by the goslings, crossly retorts 'Don't you know, mother, how difficult it is to mind the goslings?'

It is impossible to show all that a child gains by taking part in his parents' daily work. It would be even more advantageous if parents would make more use of this association for the instruction of their children later on.

The gardener's child wants to help to weed, so the father teaches him to distinguish hemlock from parsley by noticing the difference in the brightness and smell of the leaves... A child stands at the forge watching his father strike the red-hot iron, and his father teaches him that heat makes the iron more malleable but also makes it expand, and he demonstrates this by failing to push the heated iron rod through a hole which it had entered easily earlier on. A child stands by the scales in the shop; his father shows him that one scale always goes down when he puts more on to it or takes something off the other scale, and that the scales are always level if there is an equal weight in each, but he does this not through words which convey no concept to the child but by letting him put weights on and off the scale himself... So the grocer teaches his son that coffee is the kernel of a plant, and when next they go for a walk points out where and how he can see all kinds of seeds and grains which can be treated and sold growing in the fields...

So in country and city, in the works of Nature and man, and in all the occupations of men, the child naturally guides his father, and the father guides the child in his constant search for activity of mind and body. It is quite possible for anyone to establish connections between his own sphere of knowledge and that of others, no matter how different the points at which they begin or converge. Every trade and occupation offers a starting point for the acquisition of all human knowledge. Notice how much the farmer's child can learn simply from his father's cart or plough, or the merchant's son from the multiplicity of things in which his father deals. These are genuine forms of knowledge and insight such as a child will afterwards learn at school only with the greatest difficulty, if at all, and which result from his life of work and play at home with his family.

The child feels this so intensely that he stays near his father wherever he goes and whatever he does. The father should never push him away or show impatience with his persistent questions, for with every harsh word he destroys a growing point in his child's life. But he should tell the child only what he cannot find out for himself. It is, of course, easier for the child to have an answer given by someone else, even if it is one he only half hears and understands, but it is far more valuable and stimulating for him to find it out for himself. So a father should not answer all his child's questions straightaway but should put him in the way of finding the answer as his ability and experience increase.

Parents should reflect on the pleasures they may derive from fulfilling their duties, and fathers in particular should do so, for they are most directly concerned with the guidance of the child at the later stage. Nothing can bring us greater pleasure than teaching our children and living with them. We can expect no greater satisfaction than that which comes when we are occupied with our children, and we shall nowhere find greater relaxation than in the circle of our family where we can create so much pleasure for ourselves.

If we could see a father's quiet happiness in his family life, which we can merely indicate here, we should be profoundly impressed with the truth of these statements. If such a father were to define the principles on which he acts he might say, 'I think that it is of the first importance in educating children to lead them early in their lives to the habit of concentrated thought.' That they should be kept working and active in these early years is to him so obvious that he would not think it worth mentioning. Besides, the child who learns to think will also work hard. This is a precept which needs to be borne in mind by those of us who let our children become aimless and inactive.

If we look critically at our association with our children we see that it is dead. This is a hard saying but it is certainly true. Our surroundings have no life for us; with all our knowledge we are empty, empty for our children. Almost everything we utter is hollow, without life or substance. Only in the few rare instances where our statements are based on an intuitive perception of life and Nature can we have any pleasure in their reality. We must, therefore, make haste to give life to ourselves and our children and, through them, give meaning to our speech and life to our surroundings. We must really live with them and they with us. As yet the language of our relationship is dead, for our words have no meaning—they are husks without kernel, puppets without life, counters without value.

Our surroundings are a mass of things which crush rather than uplift us, for there is no quickening word which would give them sense and meaning. We are insensitive to the significance of what we say, for all our talk is ineffective, made up of concepts which have no foundation in genuine observation or creative effort. It does not arise from life. It is like the book from which we learnt it by rote at third or fourth hand. Our language is so empty and meaningless because we have no feeling for what we say. For this reason, and for this reason alone, the life of ourselves and our children is so poor, since our language does not arise from a life rich in observation and creativity and our words contain no experience of that which they describe. We hear the sound, but receive no image, see no effect.

Let us then secure for our children that which we lack

ourselves. Let us transfuse from their lives into ours that vital creative energy of child life which we have lost. Let us learn from our children. Let us attend to the knowledge which their lives gently urge upon us and listen to the quiet demands of their hearts. Let us live for our children; then will their lives bring us joy and peace, and we shall ourselves begin to grow into wisdom.

4 *Pedagogics of the Kindergarten*

(i) *A New Year's Meditation*

W. Lange, *Friedrich Fröbels gesammelte pädagogischen Schriften*, II, 4–10

'Come, let us live for our children.'

This is indeed a call to life. As we stand at the frontier of a new year it focuses all our aspirations. It unifies our own life in itself and as part of the life of mankind, and it makes us one with the whole of creation and with the creator, the source of all life, who said, 'Let us make man in our own image.'

'Come, let us live for our children.'

Clear thought always seeks to reveal itself in action, and the practical application of our resolution to express life in all its aspects and to live for our children is an institution which will promote family life and educate the nation and all mankind. It will do this by encouraging the child's impulse to activity, investigation and creative work. It will be an institution where children instruct and educate themselves and where they develop and integrate all their abilities through play, which is creative self-activity and spontaneous self-instruction. We have in mind primarily families and schools for the care of little children, but our appeal refers also to primary and elementary schools and, indeed, to every person who aims at full and complete development. Already many families in Germany, Switzerland and North America have joined in accomplishing the ideals expressed in this appeal.

This paper is published mainly to explain and introduce this institution and so it begins with an explanation of basic principles.

The development and formation of the whole future life of each being is established at the beginning of his existence. His felicitous growth and his effectiveness depend entirely on the understanding of this first stage. In childhood man is like the plant's flower or the tree's blossom; he is a manifestation of mankind's ceaseless rebirth. As a bud is connected with the whole tree—its branch and trunk, root and crown—and so with earth and sky, and as in the course of its growth it is an integral part of the whole universe, so a man lives in communion with Nature, with mankind and with the whole spiritual order of things. He shares the life that is common to all.

The ability of a human being to grow in felicity to his full power and to achieve his destiny depends solely on a proper understanding of him in childhood. He must be understood not only in his nature but also in his relationships, and treated in ways which are appropriate.

Man is a created being and as such is both a member of a whole and also himself a whole; he is both a part and a whole. On the one hand he is a member of the created universe and on the other he is a complete being, since his creator's nature, which is a unity in itself, lives in him.

This characteristic of living and creative force which is basic in man is revealed in his impulse to create shape and form. It is seen in the child's need to occupy himself in observing things, taking them to pieces and then reassembling them. The child who is encouraged to do this finds his needs fully satisfied and at the same time he is revealing his own nature.

In the family he is to be seen again as both an individual and an essential member of a living group. Only within the entity of the family is it possible for him to become a whole person.

The child fully develops his driving need for creative activity only if the family, which is the vehicle of his existence, makes it possible for him to do so. His need for activity should be fostered within the family and he should be given the means to satisfy this impulse. Our endeavour, and indeed all genuine education, has reference to this. Our purpose is to make it possible for a man to develop from his earliest days freely and independently as a whole person, as an individual being in harmony with the whole of life. We wish to enable him to educate and instruct himself, recognising and revealing both his individuality and his part in the living universe.

Furthermore, it is in the life of the family that the child first finds love. The whole nature of the parents' love for the child is shown in their concern to encourage and develop his creative impulses. We must regard man throughout his life as a creative being and enable him to work independently; so he may from childhood extend his knowledge of himself in his relation to the creator and to all creation, and manifest his awareness of the universal presence of God in himself and in all things. The enlightenment which this demands is developed in him as he uses his power to observe and work creatively.

We see, then, that the encouragement of this impulse meets the demands of the circle of relationships in which the child is set. God reveals himself in the physical universe as life, in mankind as love, and in the wisdom of the spirit as light. So the child manifests and realises his essential being. In his life on earth he is connected with the world of Nature; in this respect he is to be regarded as a being bound and fettered, subject to impulse, sensual, alive only in a physical sense. In his mind and spirit he is a child of God and as such he is free; he is so made as to have an intuitive awareness of his nature, and of his own volition he seeks unity in his life—in this respect he is a thoughtful and perceptive being, capable of knowledge and wisdom. In his own particular existence he is united with all mankind through love; here he is to be regarded as a being struggling from bondage and chains to freedom, from disconnectedness to the unity of consciousness, from isolation to unification and peace. To attain such ends which he passionately desires he lives a life of constant effort, happy in the thought that this harmony will eventually be found.

A man becomes a whole person as he becomes conscious of all the conditions and relationships of his life and lives up to their demands. Then he is able to fulfil all his obligations as a human being.

As creative activity is fostered in the child he must be regarded as a living, loving and perceptive being. The unity of his life and its many different circumstances and relationships must be taken into account, and he must be accepted for what he is, what he has, and what he will become. He himself must see the unity which pervades the world around him. Only in this way can man develop as he really is, both as an integral whole compounded of manifold parts and as himself a part of the life of the universe.

This institution, therefore, is based on the understanding and fostering of man's nature and on the recognition of his need to be active and constructive. Its aim is to be a living whole—a tree in itself, as it were. Moreover, the intention is to establish ways in which children may be employed and taught, such as are founded on the circumstances of man's life and his relation to Nature. If these methods are from the outset progressively applied, then the child will develop all his powers and be at one with himself, with Nature and with the laws of life.

(ii) *Plan of an institution which will educate children by fostering their impulse to creative activity*

Lange, II, 11–17

If our venture is to be worthwhile, it must be consistent with the stage of general development now attained and with the level at present reached by human reason. We must connect our endeavour with an all-embracing, fundamental idea. We must perceive the meaning of life and make this our starting point. Here, therefore, it must be our concern to explain the principle which underlies the institution.

At present there is an endeavour to gain greater freedom of development and determination for the individual self. Those who are striving to achieve this are trying to discover the unity and coherence that exist among separate and diverse entities, the synthesis of opposites, the essential nature of being in the objects of perception, the spirit within the form. The individual is trying to achieve conscious understanding of himself and of life in its basic unity and immense diversity and, in the light of such understanding, to act from his own choice and in conformity with the harmony that obtains throughout the universe.

This is the character of mankind's present phase of development. Unless we would cripple our children's lives both now and for the future we must educate them in accordance with the demands of their nature and with the present stage of human growth. Therefore the present time makes upon the educator and all those who have charge of children an inescapable demand—they must grasp children's earliest activities and understand their impulse to make things and to be freely and personally active; they must encourage their desire to instruct themselves as they create, observe and experiment.

As yet little is done to meet this demand. Many wish to do so but all too often lack both really suitable media and the essential skill and knowledge. Also children's occupations and play material are not appreciated in their true significance and context; consequently they can have little interest or meaning for older people, who tend to regard any effort to foster children's play as a waste of time.

The aim of this institution is to make the needs and demands of the child's world correspond to the present stage of mankind's development and to provide parents and other educators with appropriate plays and means of occupation, i.e. of education, and so to manifest the advantages and general expedience of our appeal.

Therefore, let us live for our children.

The plan of the institution is primarily to provide

games and means of occupation such as meet the needs of parent and child, educator and pupil, and possess interest and meaning for adults as they share children's play or observe children sympathetically and intelligently.

The purpose and character of these plays may be described as follows: They are a coherent system, starting at each stage from the simplest activity and progressing to the most diverse and complex manifestations of it. The purpose of each one of them is to instruct human beings so that they may progress as individuals and as members of humanity in all its various relationships. Collectively they form a complete whole, like a many-branched tree, whose parts explain and advance each other. Each is a self-contained whole, a seed from which manifold new developments may spring to cohere in further unity. They cover the whole field of intuitive and sensory instruction and lay the basis for all further teaching. They begin by establishing spatial relationships and proceed to sensory and language training so that eventually man comes to see himself as a sentient, intelligent and rational being and as such strives to live. From observation of Nature and life in all its phenomena they lead us to perceive that there is always an inner coherence and that the material and spiritual worlds are one. As older people participate in these plays so they will find their own lives enlarged and invigorated.

We shall give with each play full instructions in the text. We shall describe the method and purpose of each play, explain its place in the whole system, give directions in word and illustration for its use, show its basis in educational theory, and reveal its significance for the discovery, observation and growth of the individual self.

The second intention of our plan is to satisfy the demands of man's present stage of development and to instruct adults in its achievement. We shall comment on each phase of instruction so that its higher significance may be seen and man may understand himself in his essential being, in the unfolding of his personality and in the totality of his relationships.

I am deeply convinced that man, faithful to his own nature and to the higher claims of humanity of which he is a part, is striving to learn to understand and express life's real coherence, and this in spite of the fragmentary character of his life and the constant quest for that which is immediately useful to himself. In this institution we hope to answer a real need of the present age and give an education such as corresponds to the deepest wishes of parents and educators—though of these they may not themselves have reached awareness.

(iii) *The child's life: his first actions*

Lange, II, 18–24

As a kernel of seed-corn dropped from the plant has life within it which develops of itself, so the child lives and grows in close relationship to the whole of life. The child's life in its awakening is first shown in activity. He is active in expressing his inner life in outward form, and so he is busy noticing and reacting to the outer world, trying to master it and understand it. Therefore, early in his life there is apparent an activity associated with sensitivity and observation which indicates a latent understanding of himself and a growing awareness of his capacity.

The nature of man as a being destined to attain self-consciousness is to be found in the special sort of

7-2

activity which children show after they are three months old; the indications of this may be slight at first but they are distinct enough to be understood. The whole of this activity can best be described as 'occupying oneself'. The child's impulse, which develops at the same time as his inner life awakens, is to occupy himself: i.e. as sensitivity and perception develop, to be physically active so as to increase his own development. As I have already said, in all his relationships man finds his needs fully satisfied if in childhood his purposeful activity has been taken care of and his impulse to occupy himself encouraged, and this, I am convinced, must be the basis for education. This impulse is consistent with man's creativity: he acts, feels and thinks. It is appropriate to his nature: he has abilities, he perceives and understands, he grows in consciousness of himself, he becomes a self-determining creature. So the whole human being, all humanity, life itself, are comprehended in this impulse to activity...

There is a world of difference between the helplessness of the new-born baby and his ability later on to help himself as will power and capacity for action develop. In fact, helplessness should stimulate this energy; it is by triumphing over obstacles that man's freedom of consciousness is secured and his likeness to God enhanced. The child's life soon comes to turn on these two pivots—his helplessness and his own will or intention—and he finds the point of balance in his own activity, in the employment of his own powers.

For the educator here is the key to the child's life and to phenomena which are so difficult both to deal with and to explain. This key opens the door on the light and shadow of the child's life and on those aspects of it which often seem contradictory.

As he resolves his problems by activity so the child soon establishes tendencies and habits—often from inertia or convenience—which are easily recognisable and worth noticing. In forming a judgement about a child one should also keep in mind the fact that every aspect tends to engender its antithesis. Moreover, a child will accustom himself to an environment when he has freedom of action and will be freely active where his surroundings are familiar.

It is, therefore, just as important that those who have charge of children should watch how they accommodate themselves to their environment and notice the cause and sequence of the habits they acquire as that they should promote their desire for activity. It may indeed be said that the child's ability to adapt to his environment and identify with it is evidence of his desire for activity. And this applies even if he seems completely passive, since he may be so in order to give freer play to the workings of his mind.

Imitation is another significant development which also arises from free activity. Early in the child's life all these characteristics appear in close association; they give us important information and point clearly to the correct way to treat him. They are each and all essential to the study of children and, taken together, they reveal educational aims such as correspond to the child's essential nature. These are that the child should maintain himself as an independent being who is yet involved in the whole of life—for this is what he feels and finds himself to be; that he should use and develop his limbs and senses and make himself free so that by his own effort he gains greater independence and depth of personality; that he should get to know his environment and convince himself of its independent existence.

A child who is healthy and physically comfortable will first employ himself in observing his surroundings, taking in the outer world, and playing, i.e. working out his own life for himself. This dual activity of taking in the outer world and living out one's inner life is fundamental to his nature. As a human being he is meant to reach knowledge of what life is and to live in conformity to its demands. He does this by examining and accepting the external world and by giving expression to the world within him. As he compares these worlds he comes to see that they are one.

To receive the external world man has his senses. To give material expression to the world of his mind he has his physical powers and attributes. To grasp the unity of the spirit he has his intuition, his heart and mind, his spiritual awareness.

Physical and sensory training is, therefore, important even in the early years. In the development of the child's mind the kind of observation which he makes of the outer world and the way in which he accepts it are clearly also important. The child's use of experience, the insight and knowledge he derives from it, and consequently the way in which he expresses and reveals his nature depend on the kind of play and occupations which he chooses. As man's life in all its apparent diversity is a complete whole it is possible to see and recognise in the baby, even if only by the faintest signs, all the mental processes which emerge as dominant later on. If anyone doubts their existence in the baby, who is apparently so helpless and unaware, I reply that if they were not already there in his life they could never be developed from it. On this Christ's love for children was founded. This is why the mother treats the child from the moment of his birth as a being possessed of understanding and power. Nothing can emerge if the germ of it is not already there.

The child has a vague apprehension of his own conscious life and of the life around him; so he tries out his power, estimates it, finds out what he can do on his own. In the baby's life and activity this is the starting point, as it is also the highest limit of his achievement.

As soon as the child is able to use his limbs and senses and to distinguish and identify sounds we should try to find for him a suitable object which he can grasp and hold. The child is aware of the unity which exists in all diversity and the object should express this. The child should see his own life reflected in its self-containment and its movement—though his awareness may not be at any conscious level—and be able to try out his ideas by means of such an object. This plaything is the sphere or ball.

(iv) *The sphere and the cube: the second plaything*

Lange, II, 54, 70–3, 76–8

We have already commented on the importance of correct understanding of the child's nature and of his relations with his surroundings, and it is no less important that the relation of the child's play and playthings to himself, to his immediate environment, to the world of Nature and to God should be understood. The child will live a full and happy life if both his general development and his play harmonise with the life that is in all things. The plays and occupations which we have planned at the second stage of play with the sphere and cube are based on the endeavour to achieve this...

In the use of the second gift, I venture to say, the child seems to have a vague idea in his own mind of man's nature and purpose—which is to analyse and balance the antithetical elements in his own life, those elements which are permanent and stable and those which progress and change.

The child puts the spherical and rectangular forms together into the shape of the human body, and he can see that the doll so made looks like a baby in arms. But when he takes delight in his doll he then invests it with life. His joy has a deeper foundation than is generally supposed, for it goes beyond mere perception of an external resemblance and a similarity of form in a doll and a baby. He develops as a human being as he plays with the doll because, in doing so, he objectifies his own nature and reveals it to himself and to those who are watching him. Later on the differences in attitude and aim between the boy and the girl become clear. The boy will play longer with the sphere and the cube as separate and distinct things while the girl prefers the single complete toy, the doll. The boy feels that he must master the outer world, the girl that she is meant to foster life. This soon becomes more obvious. The girl sees the spherical and angular forms put together in the doll, her play-child; the boy sees them in his mother's yardstick or his father's walking-stick which he uses as a hobby-horse.

We must ask parents to observe all expressions of his inmost being which the child's life reveals. To the objection that only the mature mind can reflect and discriminate I say yet again that if this power of thought were not there to influence the child it could not emerge later on. The whole life of the tree, surely, is in each germinating seed, and in every child and in every one of its activities the effect of all human life is there.

If only my words could achieve their object! If only

we considered the child's life in its true inward significance and its relation to the totality of life and saw childhood as the most important stage in man's entire development!

In the play already described the sphere was mostly introduced as something self-evident which also spoke of itself to the child. It is natural that each object should, as it were, speak to man and link its life with his. Indeed, man's whole development requires that his surroundings speak to him clearly in their outward appearance and that in childhood he is enabled to see and understand what it is they are saying. So in her words and songs the mother tries to express this and bring the life of his environment closer to him so that in it he will feel and find himself. In play his surroundings and eventually the whole world of Nature become a mirror of his own self. This cannot begin too early, for in this way, as soon as awareness begins, an interaction grows up between the child's life and the life of Nature. As he gives form to material things so he may see in them again his own life which he is shaping...

The second plaything, as indeed all and every play with the child, is significant for the close connection which it establishes between the child and his mother. As they play she cannot help noticing that the love which so intimately unites her to him has various elements. There is her love for the child, her love for the medium of play and its effect, and her love for the great life-whole of which she and the child are both a part. The child's feelings are somewhat the same. He comes to see the objects of play as silent expressions of love; he perceives his mother's love for him, and through the plaything he comes to feel that the external world to which it belongs is full of life and love.

Another point to notice is that it is actually the degree of satisfaction experienced in this play which determines the style and character and sets the keynote of his future life. So the child is to be assured of satisfaction and contentment of mind, and this he will have if people reveal to him their own happiness and treat the objects around him with respect for their real nature. He will begin to feel the interdependence of love with the necessary and natural order of things and will eventually see that this is the true condition of all satisfaction. Equipped with this real treasure in the heart, he can, if it should be required, even in youth be surrendered to the world. If this contentment is deeply grounded, all the other blessings of life will follow.

It is a particular purpose of this play to give such contentment and stability to the child, but in all our provision for him there are three considerations to bear in mind. It must be done in order to establish unity in his life; it must be done in union and agreement with the medium of employment; it must be done so that a higher level of union with the whole of life may be established and proclaimed. In this context I use the word 'union' where elsewhere I have spoken of 'love'.

These and other games were devised, therefore, to help the child to be happy and to prevent him becoming bored and dejected, as easily becomes a habit if he cannot or may not handle the objects around him and finds no outlet for his vital instincts. Bored, he is a burden to himself; unsatisfied, he appears sulky and demanding. From such experiences it can never be too soon to save him, and it can be done if his impulse to activity is understood and encouraged.

(v) *The third plaything*

Lange, II, 85–7, 88–9

It is important to search for the real, hidden causes of a child's actions. It is this which secures to parents their children's respect and love, particularly if they allow them to develop freely by themselves within the limits of their strength and ability, letting them know they are protected, without, however, making them feel the guiding hand. The child does not want to be left entirely alone; he likes to feel that a careful eye is always being kept on him. His desire for protection of this kind is something that parents should foster, for he naturally comes to the unity of all life through such a unity of life within the family.

Parents should start to care for the child's mind as well as for his body from the moment of his birth. The child will dimly realise that this sort of attention is being given to him, and will soon have the idea that care for his physical well-being has a wider reference. So we must insist that attention to the life of the child's mind be given long before it finds expression and the delicate feeling for it is disturbed or blocked by any outside influence, for the child's perceptions which all too often elude us usually go far beyond any outward manifestation. Therefore, when we think we are exerting an influence on the child it is frequently much too late. Parents are often only too anxious to find words to revive the child's sense of love and respect, but what is the use of exhortation when there is no longer any community of feeling? It is just as possible to establish purity of heart as it is to build up habits of physical cleanliness.

As soon as possible the child's life should be warmed

by the realisation that there is a beneficent purpose in everything that is done for him. If his feeling that people care for his inner life leads him to see himself as a whole and also as part of a higher unity, then love and gratitude will truly develop in his heart. It would be unnatural if in these circumstances he did not show some awareness of the unity and source of all life which manifests itself in love.

These games are devised to bring such enrichment to parents and children. There is one further point. If we look at life as it is we see that the adult world is now more removed than ever from that of childhood, and that this has occurred because family life and the treatment of childhood no longer correspond to the insight we have gained into the life of Nature and its postulates for mankind. But if this is now to be remedied we hope it will be achieved through the care for childhood such as we have in mind. Certainly this is the aim of our games which are based on the underlying unity of all life...

The third plaything which we give to the child is devised to make diversity of appearance and structure yet clearer to him. Suppose we try to observe what a child between the ages of one and three is moved to do and what he needs. If we put ourselves in the corner of the living-room or at the table where he plays, we can unobtrusively watch how he first examines the colour and shape of any object which he handles. He will feel it, move it about in his hands, and then try to reshape it or take it to pieces. He will be trying to find out new things about it or new ways of using it. If he does take it apart, then we see how he tries to rebuild or reshape it and how he goes on doing this for quite a long time. This tells us what we have to give to the child for the next plaything—it must be something solid which can easily be pulled apart and just as easily put together again; it must be both simple and multiform. So from the material to hand we devise the divided cube, our third gift to the child.

(vi) *Movement*

Lange, II, 182-7

All man's activity expresses purpose, relationship. Every act is the furtherance of some end or the representation of some idea, but there must be a medium of expression in material form. For his purposes the child needs something as a means of expression—it need be no more than a bit of wood or stone—and so we give him the ball, the sphere, the cube and other playthings so that he may be initiated into the handling of play material. Each of these requires of the child further attempts at activity and movement on his own. So far, however, we have not specially considered the plays of movement, for, as I have explained, the method proper to child development is one of inference from the general to the particular, from whole to part. But now that we have reached this point in our explanation of play material we can do so.

It is not enough simply to give the child material appropriate to his powers when we see signs that they are developing. We must track down the inner process of growth and meet its demands. Though the real source of all the child's actions lies deep in his nature, he has the strongest desire to see his thoughts given visible form in order himself to come to an understanding of their nature and purpose. He would like to see his inner activity through this mirror so that he can further determine his life in accordance with what he sees. This process of objectifying himself, or mirroring his inner life, is of the highest importance if he is to come to self-consciousness and learn to organise and master himself. The child must first see and grasp his own life in an objective manifestation before he can know and understand it in himself. This course of development is prescribed by Nature and by the child's own being, and therefore the true educator must most closely follow it. My games, play methods and procedure are all aimed at bringing educators to a recognition of this fact.

The educator should not regard the manifestations of children's activity as external and isolated, but always as affecting or arising from their inner life. In this connection the children are our teachers. Sometimes we see a small child moving happily about, skipping and jumping and throwing his arms around when he sees some moving object. This is not merely an expression of his delight in seeing the movement but rather an effect of the mental activity which it releases and stimulates. Also, if we observe even younger children, we see that they are busy following any moving object with their eyes and trying to find out what is causing it to move. In the same way the educator looks for the causes of a child's activity. His most important consideration must always be the child's own nature. He may get some clues by interpreting isolated actions, but this is not the way to achieve the proper aim of education, which is comprehension of the whole man and the fullest possible realisation of his essential nature throughout his life from childhood onwards. An education which fails to keep this purpose in view can make no claim to be worthy of man.

After this introduction we go on to consider the start-

ing point and progression of the plays of movement...
The germ of all these plays lies in the use of the first
plaything, the ball...As the ball moves gently, then
rolls and runs, so we see the baby begin to stir and
move. The game called 'The child wants to go, too'
originated in this way. The child finds pleasure in the
movement of body or limbs because it excites a feeling
of power. Simply to walk is a pleasure because he is
conscious that he can move, get from one place to
another, and so grasp or reach some object. So if we
wish to lay a good foundation for his activities later on,
we must carefully watch his earliest movements and
encourage all these reactions. We should therefore see
that, when he starts to walk, he uses all his strength so
that he is gaining control over body and limbs and
learning to use them for definite purposes. We do indeed see this in the child's first attempts; holding his
mother's hand, he will frequently make for some object
or will avoid some impediment. It may be that his
effort to reach it is more often caused by his need for
support, but we also see that it gives him pleasure to be
actually near it; he likes to feel, touch, hold, perhaps
even push it. When he gets near he hops up and down
and even beats on it to assure himself of its reality.

At this stage it is a good thing to give names to the
objects—'This is a chair, a table, a flower', and 'This
is the seat, the leg, the corner of the chair' and 'This
chair is hard, its seat is smooth, its corner sharp'. The
point of giving these words is not to develop his powers
of speech but to help him to understand and respond
to the object. But such a rich store of experience is
bound also to develop the capacity for speech. Since the
child's mind has become more active, speech will
naturally break forth of itself, as it were.

To help the child to this store of rich experience it is well to let him pull himself up by means of the objects and walk round them. Each fresh thing is a new discovery in the child's small and yet rich world. If it is a chair he can go round it and stand in front or to the side; if it is a bench or wall then he cannot go behind it. So the care of little children will come to be seen as a stimulating and satisfying task. Even the smallest child who has only just started walking likes to wander around; he loves to change the position of all the different objects and so come to understand himself and the world around him. Each walk is for him a voyage of discovery and each new object is an America, a new world to explore.

(vii) *The child's love of drawing*

Lange, II, 352–60, 367–9

A healthy child is always active. What does this mean? He wants to show the desires hidden within him; therefore, as his ideas and opinions alter, as the images of his soul change, his creative acts are modified.

But what is the cause of all the child's activity? It is life, as life is the first cause of all existence in God. He feels that not only life but also consciousness is in everything. It is a sign of his affinity with God the creator that not only does he regard all his surroundings as containing life hidden within them but also that he invests with life all the things which he makes or sees. These become a kitten, a mouse, a bird or a fish. Lambs are seen in white stones or in the flowers of poplar and willow trees. Sticks represent trees, blocks of wood persons. Even his own fingers must become something else such as fishes or birds. So the child, himself an organic unity, always at first represents objects as also organic unities. It is not until later when his critical sense and creative power have increased that he makes comparisons and divisions.

In what sequence and in what way does the child begin to manifest this formative power? He uses his own limbs, often his whole body, to represent different things by putting fingers or hands together. Then he tries to express his ideas in solid, tangible objects. He first examines them to see whether they stand on their own, whether they are mobile and flexible. He finds out whether they can be taken apart and put together again. So balls, blocks of wood and stones are his first play-things. In using them he testifies to his inner life; his actions are evidence of creative impulses and an indica-tion of their nature. Even more important is the evidence which his attempts to draw provide later on.

Probably in his second and definitely in his third year he looks for other play material. First, there is plastic material—soft clay, wet sand, water, and air to drive and turn things. Second, there are less solid objects such as small flat pieces of wood, smooth paper, or sticks and threads. Last, there is a choice of dry sand, sawdust, glass which can be moistened and breathed on, and objects such as slates, slate-pencils, paper, chalk or crayons. So the child takes pleasure in drawing and painting, and both are essential for his education. Music is especially important, since the sounds which he pro-duces in singing or by striking bells or glass or metal serve to give creative expression to feelings and ideas.

We see, therefore, that as the play material becomes less tangible so there is greater advance in creative expression. Plastic materials give more scope for expression than the solid objects; with sticks the child can only make rough outlines, but he can give a better picture by drawing in sand or on dimmed glass and an even better one if he uses paper and pencil. It is, however, the transient sound in its rhythm and melody which is the highest expression and communication of feeling. It is through the spirit that man recognises himself as a creative being, a child of God.

We see that the child's whole activity from his first spontaneous movement to the time when, at the age of seven or eight, his power of expression has been achieved is caused by the effort to externalise his thoughts and to assimilate his surroundings. It is a question of understanding and revealing his thoughts in an actual created thing, since the living spirit is the determining factor which conditions the material he uses. Yet his power to create is still limited. He should not, however, be prevented from using it; if he is properly educated he will always feel that his capacity is adequate to his aim. His limitations serve to strengthen his desire by challenging his power, so he must not be disturbed in his attempts, however fruitless they seem to be, for his power to create is increasing. As a rule he will choose to practise on material which he will eventually be able to use for his purpose.

Children need encouragement as growing plants need warmth and light, and they must have their parents' love and understanding. As soon as the child can speak he is asking, 'Draw me a house', 'Paint a bird, a flower, for me', 'Tell me a story', 'Tell me the story about the birds who loved their mother'. As soon as he can get hold of any plastic material he tries to carry his ideas into tangible shapes and forms.

In all that he does, even in his play with stones and bits of wood, he is painting and drawing himself, as it were. But it is painting and drawing in the strict sense, even if it is only drawing in the earth or on glass that he has breathed on, that attract him most of all. These are the most satisfying means of expression since they give him power to represent the star, the flower, the tree in the wood, the bird singing in the tree or spreading its wings in the air.

The child's need to make use of the most pliable and delicate material in his creative work is in accordance with the activity and phenomena of Nature which creates from light, air, water, earth and dust. Here also his aim is not to be seen as something separate and isolated but as an integral means by which he assures himself that he is a part of the whole of life. We must respect the child's desire to affirm his powers of expression through these objects, since he is proving that he is both a creative being and also a part of the whole circle of life. He is meant to develop in this way so that he may know the creator and the created world of Nature and become aware of himself as mediating between them through his actions. Like Nature and like God who created himself and the physical world he is destined to create the great from the small and to realise what is good and true and beautiful.

It is in drawing that the child pre-eminently shows himself to be creative because with limited control of the material and with little physical effort he can recognisably show what he wants to express. Yet so far drawing has not been generally regarded as essential, and as a result children have been deprived of one of the most effective means of their education.

Drawing is an activity which makes a demand on the whole person. Even the correct use of the hand involves the free use of the arm and therefore of the whole body.

Free skilful use of both body and mind is involved, for they are interdependent...Above all, the child must early on be allowed to realise that a free posture gives him a pleasantly relaxed feeling as well as freedom of movement and sensory perception...

The child's pleasure in drawing develops his desire to shape a whole, to recognise separate parts as constituents of a whole, and to find in opposites a common linking factor. In giving recognition to this desire he sees the growth of his creative ability and, with some idea of how shapes are created, soon starts to find out the shapes which he can make, though perhaps not yet to represent living forms. The first shapes which he makes are the first witness to his inherent creativity. So we see how radical and profound observations on life can be made on the basis of quite simple small activities, and how formation and structure can be vividly revealed to the child. Even though he cannot yet understand or describe it, the child sees objectively that he is by nature thoughtful and creative—at least his actions would lead us to think so.

In his observation the child passes from perceiving the object as a whole to considering it in its constituent parts and outlines. In drawing and in simply linking lines together he again gives expression to something that can be identified. In doing so he shows that he is determined to achieve something which he can also describe. So he establishes his creativity and in his thought and observation intuitively applies the simple rules of formation which exist in his own mind. So he comes to a recognition of himself, and finally the circle is completed and he forms himself into a living whole. Through knowing and creating his own self the child becomes a true human being. Therefore this capacity should not be released to find expression merely in indefinite creations but should be developed in conformity with the inherent formative principles of his own life.

5 Outline of a plan for founding and developing a Kindergarten

E. Hoffmann, *Fröbel. Ausgewählte Schriften*, I, 117-20

We here appeal to all German women to unite in founding and promoting a general institution where all aspects of the child's life can be fostered in the preschool period. We need their united support in this work of establishing the German Kindergarten. In a garden growing plants are cultivated in harmony with Nature under God's care and with the skilled attention of a gardener. So here children, seeds and members of humanity and the highest of all organisms, are to be brought up in understanding of themselves, God and Nature. Here we shall show and start on the way which leads to such an education. In achieving its aim this institution will meet an urgent need; it will train men and women to take care of children and educate them in their earliest years. In all confidence we invite support for this venture, for our work has already been favourably regarded by German women of all ranks.

The aim of this enterprise is to bring certainty and stability into the care of children in the earliest years, for otherwise their growth is adversely affected, and to base this care on eternal principles logically deduced and manifested in Nature, history and divine revelation.

Women will understand how important it is that the children whom they have borne with so much pain and suffering should from the beginning receive an education such as they intuitively desire for them, an education which will relate to the divine, human and natural aspects of the child's own being.

First, then, our enterprise will give a training in the care of children so as to meet the needs of children's nurses, nursery teachers, and men and women teachers in general and to train leaders, both men and women, for the various institutions which already exist in many places—crèches, play schools, industrial schools and the so-called infant schools. They are to be trained to respect the child's nature and lovingly care for his full and complete development.

The children's nurses and nursery governesses must be efficient as mediators between the life of the mother and that of the child. So they must be competent in the management of a household and also well versed in the care and guidance of children. This requires that they, and indeed all teachers, should be initiated into the nature and manner of the child's growth, inspired with respect and love for it, and made thoroughly familiar with the demands of the child's life and the form of education which will satisfy these demands. Also they should be led to know Nature and observe life in their immediate environment so that they may be qualified to guide the child to do the same.

In order that these extensive aims should be realised the teachers appointed to the institution should be men of the greatest understanding and knowledge who completely accept the whole idea on which it is based. The institution also requires the best educational equipment so that it may work within its appointed field and prepare for the schools that are to follow...

Finally, the great aim and end of the whole enterprise

is the education of a person from the earliest years through his own doing, feeling and thinking and in conformity with his own nature and relationships so that his life is an integrated whole. This will be achieved if the child's activity is rightly fostered and his essential nature developed and experienced. In such a comprehensive enterprise there is no room for anything which disturbs or might destroy such purposes. On the contrary, it must be promoted by everything which its needs demand, and in the whole scheme everything must be purposive. Not only the child's material environment but also everything which happens to him must express its reference to a higher unity of life.

IV THE CHILD AND THE SCHOOL

The major part of *The Education of Man* is devoted to an analysis of the child's development in the first years of school age and to an examination of the school in terms of the needs of his nature and the broad fields of knowledge which must be opened to him. Although there are many lengthy digressions—which are omitted in this selection— where Froebel expounds his views on themes such as the development of language, the main argument is fairly evident. This part of the book was, in practical terms, based on the educational experience of Keilhau. In intention the whole book was an appeal for general support of the principles accepted there. It was written at a time of hope when Froebel expected to be given a wider field of work, and it is linked with a number of appeals and schemes in which he sought approval for the Keilhau ideas as the basis for a national plan of education. Although he was disappointed in his expectations, especially from the Duke of Meiningen for whom he composed a plan of an educational institute,[1] Froebel never despaired of public acceptance of his pattern of educational reform.

During the period from 1831 to 1836 when he was in Switzerland he set up a school supported by the townspeople of the little town of Willisau in the canton of Lucerne, and there he wrote the *Plan of an institution for the education of the poor in the canton of Berne*. This plan is typical of the schemes of reform which he was devising at this time and reveals the scope and character of the institutions he had in mind. His chance to make a successful experiment in such a venture came in 1835 when the Bernese government gave him direction of the orphanage at Burgdorf. However, success was achieved only to be abandoned for a new ambition. It was during these years that the unrest of new ideas

[1] The Helba plan. See Lange, vol. i, pt. i, pp. 399–417.

and fresh hopes can be seen. His interest from now on was to be absorbed in the experiments which culminated in the Kindergarten.

Although Froebel always hoped for public support of his ventures, he was not primarily concerned with national systems of education. That would have been alien to his way of thought. He was concerned with the establishment of true communities, with the transformation of a people's way of life through the family—'the true root of human life'—and the school.

1 *The Education of Man: in boyhood*

E. Hoffmann, *Fröbel. Ausgewählte Schriften*, II, 58–65, 66–74, 75–84, 86–7, 90–8, 121–32, 140–2, 143–9, 251–4

As the previous stage of childhood was predominantly that of living, of the child externalizing the thoughts in his mind, so boyhood is above all the time for learning, for receiving into the mind the significance of external things.

The main requirement of the earliest period is that parents should care for the baby. Childhood, the period in which the human being asserts and develops himself as an individual, is above all the time for education. In the next stage, that of boyhood, man is involved mainly in particular relationships and in the consideration of particular things, which leads later on to the inference of their essential unity as their characteristics and connections are probed and proved. It is essentially the business of instruction to treat of particular things and their connections, and so boyhood is the period in which instruction predominates.

This instruction depends less on the nature of the human being himself than on the laws which are in the nature of things and which govern both things and men.

More significantly, it depends less on the expression of universal law within human development than on its particular appearance in everything external to man and on its manifestation in both man and material things at one and the same time. It conforms to fixed and definite conditions which are external to man, and this requires from him knowledge and awareness, discernment and control. Such giving of instruction is school in the widest sense of the word.

School, therefore, is the place where man is led to know material things according to the general and special laws inherent in them and, as he is shown particular and individual phenomena, to arrive at a realisation of their unity and universality. School age begins with boyhood, whether schooling takes place within the home or outside it, whether under the father or some other member of the family or a teacher. The term 'school' is to be understood here neither as schoolroom nor as school-keeping but as the conscious communication of items of knowledge for a deliberate purpose and in deliberate interconnection.

In the attainment of its purpose, however, human development is manifestly an unbroken whole, continuously progressing from one stage of growth to another. From the sense of relationship aroused in the baby arise inclinations and drives which form the child's disposition and emotions. From this proceeds the boy's activity of mind and will, and so the guidance and instruction of boys is mainly concerned with the development of volition. The boy's will must be made firm; it must become strong and enduring so that essential human qualities can be exercised and expressed...

The boy's education rests solely on his upbringing as

a child, for activity and strength of will grow out of activity and strength of feeling, and if the latter is undeveloped the former will be hard to attain.

The child expresses his goodness of heart and mind in an intense longing to find in the apparently separate things which he sees in profusion around him an essential unity such as he feels within himself. He longs to find in things an immaterial bond, a connecting principle, which will give them a living significance. In childhood this longing finds satisfaction in the full enjoyment of play, for in play the child is the centre of everything and all things are related to him and his life. It is in family life above all that this desire is completely satisfied, for there only can be developed in its full intensity the goodness of heart and thoughtfulness of mind which are incomparably important for every period of growth. This sense of unity is the primary condition of all human development, and every feeling of separation frustrates it. So the child refers everything to the life of the family and sees everything mirrored there.

Parents ought always to bear in mind the fact that a child regards his own family life objectively and takes it as an ideal of life; he would like to reproduce in his own existence the harmony and strength he sees there.

In the family the child sees his parents and others doing useful and productive work, and he would like to represent what he sees, for in this way he arrives at a knowledge of human potentialities and means of expression. While the little child likes activity purely for its own sake, the boy is active in working to effect a result. The child's love of activity has become in the boy an all-absorbing desire to create shape and form.

At this age the boy and girl have a great desire to

share in their parents' work. They do not want the easy occupations but the hard work which demands strength and exertion. It is at this point that parents need to be careful and sensible. By rejecting their children's help as useless and even obstructive they could suddenly destroy or dam up their creative impulses. They should never be misled into saying, 'Go away, you are only hindering me,' or 'I am in a hurry and will do it more quickly on my own.' Children who are interrupted in this way are disconcerted if they are excluded from the activity with which they had felt identified. They feel isolated and have no idea what to do with the energy which has been stimulated and which is now only a burden. So they lapse into dullness and apathy. This rejection by the parents need only happen a few times and the child no longer offers to help or share in any work; he stands around listless and bored, even when it is work in which he could quite easily participate. So we hear parents saying, 'Look at him! When he was small and couldn't help me he was always in the way, but now he just won't do anything.'

Parents need to understand that the first creative impulses arise from unconscious and unrecognised movements of the child's mind, which occur entirely without his agency and even against his will, as is seen to happen later in life also. If this drive to creative expression, especially in young people in whom it is always connected with physical effort, meets an impediment such as the parents' opposition, then a person is diminished in his own strength and, if the frustration occurs frequently, withdraws entirely into apathy. A child so mishandled does not speculate why his help is accepted at one time and rejected at another; he chooses the easier way and all the more readily gives up any attempt to help since his parents seem to make it his duty to do so. So his physical energy becomes a burden to him. If parents want their children to help them in the future, they must put themselves out to encourage the little child in his pursuits and the boy in his desire to be creatively employed. Like good seed in good soil it will repay a hundredfold. In strengthening and developing this desire they meet the child's greatest need. So they must allow him to put his energy into their work as he wishes, for this gives him an awareness and also a measure of his own strength.

In early childhood he copied the activities of the home and now he shares in the actual work. He wants to try his strength on everything so as to test and extend it. He goes with his father everywhere—to field and garden, workshop and office, forest and meadow; he helps to look after the animals and make things for the house; he shares in the chopping, sawing and piling of the wood; he goes with his father whatever it is he is doing. Question after question crowds out of his enquiring mind—how? why? when? what for?—and any passably satisfactory answer opens up a new world to him. He sees language as the instrument of communication for everything.

The healthy boy who has been simply and naturally brought up never evades an obstacle or difficulty but looks for it and overcomes it. 'Let it alone,' he will cry as his father goes to take a log out of his way, 'I'll get over it.' When he gets over it by himself, however difficult it may be, he is encouraged by the success and goes back to climb it again; soon he is jumping over it as if there were nothing in his way. As the child delighted in activity, so now the boy takes pleasure in purposive action and expresses his energy in daring and adventure.

He climbs into caves and crevices, clambers up trees and hills, searches heights and depths, and roams through fields and forests. Nothing seems difficult, nothing dangerous, when his own nature and his own mind and will prompt him to do it.

However, it is not merely the desire to use and test his strength which drives him far and wide to seek adventure. His mind in its growth requires that he looks at the diversity of things, sees the isolated unit as part of a whole, brings the remote into nearness to himself, and assimilates the range and variety of things in their totality. His aim is to enlarge his range of vision stage by stage.

To climb a new tree is for the boy to discover a new world. Everything lies clearly below him; seen from above, everything looks quite different from the usual telescoped, distorted side-view. If we could remember our joy when in childhood we looked out beyond the cramping limits of our immediate surroundings, we should not be so insensitive as to call out, 'Come down, you will fall.' One learns to protect oneself from falling by looking over and around a place as well as by physical movement, and the most ordinary thing certainly looks quite different when seen from above. Ought we not, then, to give the boy opportunities for an enlargement of his view which will broaden his thoughts and feelings? 'But he will be reckless and I shall never be free of anxiety about him.' No, the boy whose training has always been connected with the gradual development of his capacities will attempt only a little more than he has already been able to do, and will come safely through all these dangers. It is the boy who does not know his strength and the demands made on it who is likely to venture beyond his experience and run into unsuspected danger. Those boys are always the most reckless who have no constant experience of their strength and suddenly have a burst of energy when there is an opportunity to use it. Then they are likely to run into danger, especially if anyone is watching them.

Another significant development is the boy's liking for climbing into caves and crevices and wandering in dark woods and forests. He wants to seek out and find the undiscovered, see and know the unseen, uncover and possess that which exists in darkness. From such excursions he brings back rich spoils of unfamiliar stones and plants, of creatures that live in the dark—worms, beetles, spiders, lizards. 'What is this? What is its name?' Every word that we give in answer enriches his world. What one must never do is to call out as he comes along, 'Throw that horrid thing away,' or, 'Drop it, it will sting you.' If the child takes notice, he rejects something essential to himself. Later on, when you or his own common sense tells him to look at a little creature which is quite harmless, he will look away and a great deal of knowledge will be lost. On the other hand a little boy hardly six years old can tell you things about the wonderful organism and movement of a beetle which you have never noticed before. You should, of course, warn a child to be careful in handling unfamiliar creatures, but never in such a way as to make him afraid.

However, the lively boy is not always on the heights or in the depths. He is exploring everywhere and examining everything. He makes a little garden by his father's fence, maps out a river's course in the cart-track or ditch, studies the effects of the fall and pressure of water on his small water-wheel, or observes a piece of flat wood or bark as it floats on the water which he had dammed to form a pool. He has a particular liking for playing with water which reveals him to himself, as it were. For the same reason he likes to be busy with plastic materials such as sand and clay which may be called a vital element for him. He seeks to use the power he has already gained over material things so that he can now control them; everything must submit to his desire to give it shape and form.

In his increasing confidence the boy makes use of everything which suits his need and combines all sorts of things together. Every person forms his own world for himself, for the sense of one's own power soon demands possession of space and material exclusively one's own. The boy's kingdom may be only a corner of a yard or house, perhaps only a box or cupboard, a den or shed, but some place he must have to serve as a centre and point of reference for his activities, and this is best chosen by himself. If the area to be controlled is large or the project complex, this gives opportunity for a common enterprise and, if the children all put their efforts into it, they will enlarge the whole scope of the work in hand or turn individual schemes into the basis for a common activity.

It is particularly important also that boys should cultivate gardens of their own, for there they will first see their efforts leading to an organic result. The boy will see that the yield, though subject to laws of Nature which he cannot control, depends largely on the character of his work. Here his life with Nature and his curiosity about flowers and plants and other natural phenomena will be fully and variously satisfied, and his efforts will be rewarded, for children's gardens usually grow and flourish. If the boy cannot have a garden-plot of his own, he should at least have a plant or two in a box or pot, and these should be common and prolific rather than rare, delicate plants. The child or boy who has cared for another living thing, even though it is of a lower order, is more easily led to care for his own life. The care of plants will in other ways also satisfy his desire to watch living creatures, for he will see birds and butterflies and beetles coming nearby.

If we consider the plays and occupations of boys at this age we see that they do not all aim at the representation of things; many are simply for the exercise, trial and display of strength. Yet this play always has a distinctive character related to the boy's inner life and possessing a definite, conscious purpose. Unlike the child's play which is activity for its own sake, the boy's playing aims at the representation of thought and experience, and this feature of his play is intensified as he grows older; this is evident even in activities involving physical movement such as running, racing, boxing or wrestling and in games of war or hunting. It is not only physical energy that is strengthened; the vigour of intellectual and moral qualities is developed to perhaps an even greater degree. In a group of boys playing such games the virtues of justice, moderation, self-control, comradeship and fairness are to be seen. The boys may also show harder qualities in their courage and coolness and in their rejection of ease and indolence. To visit such playgrounds is like a new breath of life. Here we can see the subtler virtues also, such as tolerance, care and encouragement of those who are weaker or younger or who are new to the game. It is true that there is many a rough word or act, but the sense of power has first to exist before it can be trained or become controlled. The boy has a sharp sense of the inner meaning of an action and is capable of accurate, even harsh, judgement of those who are or claim to be his equals.

There should be a communal playground in every locality. The results would be excellent for the whole community since boys of this age play together at every opportunity, and their games develop a sense of common interests and a respect for the laws and obligations of society. The boy seeks to see and feel himself in his companions, measure himself by them, and come to know himself through them. Games of this sort directly train him for life and awaken many moral and social virtues.

The boy cannot spend all his leisure time in the open air, however, for seasons and circumstances may make it impracticable. Therefore, since he should never be inactive, all kinds of indoor occupations, especially constructive work with paper and cardboard, modelling and so on, should be included in his training.

However, there is in the boy an innate need which these occupations do not meet. He cannot be entirely satisfied by life in the present, however rich and full. From his experience he infers the past and wants to know of it so as to find the cause and reason of present phenomena. He wants the evidence of the past to tell its own story. Can we not all remember our longing to be told the story of old walls and towers, monuments and columns which we had seen in the hills or by the roadside, and our feeling that these objects might reveal to us information about themselves and the circumstances of their time? The boy wants those who are older and have greater experience and knowledge to tell him of these things, and he comes to need tales and legends of all kinds and also historical stories. This desire, especially at first, is so strongly felt that, if stories are not told to them, boys try to satisfy it themselves. We have all seen a group of them gathered round the one whom they have chosen as story-teller for his good memory and vivid imagination and noticed how intently they listen if they find the story is to their liking.

Even so, the boy's contemporary world contains much that he cannot explain, yet wants to have explained; many things are silent that he would hear speak, many are without the life that he would give them. He desires others to explain and make these things speak to him; he wants to have put into words his vague intuition that there is a living coherence in all things. Yet other people are rarely, if ever, able to gratify this wish, and so his desire grows for fables and fairy tales which attribute speech and reason to speechless objects; the fable does so within the limits of human relations and worldly phenomena while the fairy tale goes beyond them. If we observe the boy at this age we clearly see that he will contrive to make up tales and fables, which he will either work out in his own mind or relate for the delighted entertainment of his companions. To us who are observing him these stories vividly reveal what is unconsciously going on deep in the mind of the young story-teller.

The boy wants to find in the words of others the means of expressing his own feelings for which as yet he has no words. He is glad to find phrases, especially in song, which give expression to emotions such as his joy in springtime or his sense of power, which he is not yet old or experienced enough to put into words. The cheerful and happy boy loves to sing, for in his songs he feels himself really alive and expresses his sense of growing power as he wanders through the valley and over the hill.

The boy is enthralled by the longing to understand himself. We see him always drawn back to clear living water in his play, since he sees himself and his soul's image there and hopes to understand his own nature. Play has for him the same significance as the water in brook or lake or as the pure air and clear expanse of the mountain top; it is for his life a mirror of the challenges which are to come. Therefore boy and youth in their play seek out that which presents difficulty and struggle.

The longing to know the past draws the boy again and again to the study of old buildings; the desire to know Nature draws him to flowers and plants, and he expresses his emotions in his songs. Much of his behaviour is significant for its revelation of the life of his mind, and so gives it symbolic form. Both now and in the future parents would find that it would benefit themselves and their children if they accepted this symbolism and considered their children's lives in its context. Then they would be bound in a living relationship with the children and would find that present and future are woven into a living whole.

Such is the ideal life of a boy. Fortunately it is still to be found wherever children are brought up naturally, and it is sometimes realised more splendidly and fully than has been here described. Yet when we turn to the real lives of most of them as, however incompletely, they are revealed and look at their activities at home and school and at their relationships within their family and among their companions, we must frankly admit that the picture is quite different. We find children who are obstinate, insolent, physically and mentally lazy, self-indulgent, vain, conceited, self-assertive and demanding. They behave in an unfriendly or unchildlike way, have no inclination to work or even to play, and reveal emptiness and superficiality, disobedience and disregard of all religion. If we look for the sources of these and many other undeniable faults we find ultimately two causes. First, there may have been a complete failure to develop the varied aspects of the child's nature. Secondly, the necessary and natural course of his development may have been arbitrarily disturbed so that early in his life the original good powers have been misdirected and perverted.

Man is essentially good and possesses qualities and tendencies which are good in themselves. He is not naturally bad nor are his qualities evil, unless it is considered that the finite, the material, the transient and the physical as such are evil and that their necessary consequence, namely that it must be possible for the human being to fail if he is to achieve goodness and to be in bondage if he is to be truly free, is also evil. Yet this is inevitable since it is in temporal and separate things that eternal unity is manifested, and it is man's destiny to become conscious, rational and free. If anyone is freely and independently to choose the divine and eternal, he must have power and opportunity to accomplish that which is earthly and finite. Since God wished to make himself known in finitude, the only medium of his revelation is the finite and transient. Therefore anyone who speaks of the finite and physical as evil shows contempt for the created universe, for Nature herself—in the strict sense of the word he commits blasphemy.

It is a betrayal of humanity to say that man is neither good nor evil, and even worse to assert that he is essentially evil. This destroys God for mankind, since it destroys his work, the means by which he may be truly known, and brings into the world falsehood, the single source of all evil.

Falsehood is the primal evil, yet it does not exist of itself and will be brought to nothing since man has been created for the truth. He does not out of his own nature create falsehood. He has been created by God for the truth, and it is his failure to recognise this in himself and to see that others recognise it which is the cause of all falsehood.

Man's development on earth is meant to be a conscious, rational and harmonious growth of mind and body. He would immediately escape from all his faults, even the evil in which he is now enshrouded, if his strength of will had not been sapped by bad habits and if he were able to come to a clear knowledge of his own being. All his faults arise from the disturbance of the relationship between his character as it has developed and his innate essential being. Beneath each fault lies in origin a good quality which has been perverted and crushed, a good aspiration which has been repressed or misunderstood. Therefore the only infallible way of eradicating every defect is to try first to find and then to encourage and direct the original good tendency underlying it. The fault will eventually disappear though it may involve painful struggle—not, however, against innate evil but against habit; the effort will be successful because man will always choose the right rather than the wrong.

It cannot be denied that children today show little real gentleness, kindness, tolerance or feeling for religion. There is far too much selfishness, unfriendliness, even brutality in their lives, which is caused simply by the fact that an awareness of the bonds between them and their parents is not early aroused and that this relationship is all too often disturbed or broken. Trust and friendliness, consideration and mutual respect can only revive if the awareness of common interests, which in greater or less degree is innate in every human being, is most carefully fostered.

There are many faults also which arise simply through carelessness. When children act on an impulse, which in itself may be harmless or even praiseworthy, they can become so entirely absorbed that they have no thought for the consequences, and indeed from their own limited experience can have no knowledge of them...

Moreover it is certainly true that as a rule the child is first made bad by some other person, often by the educator himself. This can happen when everything which the child does out of ignorance or thoughtlessness or even from a keen sense of right and wrong is attributed to an intention to do evil. Unhappily there are among teachers those unfortunate persons who always see children as mischievous, spiteful, cunning little devils, whereas others see at most an over-exuberant sense of life or a situation which has got out of hand. Such people are the first to make a child, who is as yet unaware of guilt, feel guilty since they ascribe to him attitudes and actions which are quite alien. They degrade his actions, though not at first his will; they kill his spirit, for they convince him that he does not of himself possess and cannot attain spiritual life. When such life is beyond his reach, what is the use to a child of knowledge as such? What is the use of his wishing for something he cannot have? Such people believe that God will make good again the motives which they have made evil; they maintain that a child cannot attain heaven or carry a heaven in his heart without first going through guilt to get there, and this they call making him godly.

This procedure is like that of the good-natured child who handles a fly or a beetle until it is worn out and cannot move and then says, 'See how tame it is!' There are boys who seem to be badly behaved through lack of experience or control but who intensely desire to become good and capable people. Unfortunately they do in the end really go to the bad, just because their deepest striving has been all too often un-appreciated or even misjudged. Yet, if they had been understood at the right time, they would certainly in the end have grown up as very estimable persons. Children are often punished by adults for faults which they have in fact learnt from them. Punishment, especially scolding, often instils in children, or at least brings to their notice, faults which they have not possessed.

As has already been said, the boy shows in his actions his sense of the unity that pervades all things and his search for himself in material relationships. He is above all drawn to explore the hidden depths of Nature, for he feels that the satisfaction of his heart's desire is not to be found in externalities. Unfortunately we often ignore this aspect of his growth or give no support to his own efforts to develop it. At this age a boy who has been naturally brought up is really seeking, however blindly, only for the unity and ground of all things—not in the ingenuities of human thought but in God who is ever near his heart and mind and who can only be known in spirit and in truth. As he grows up the boy will find contentment only if this search has succeeded, for it is only then that he finds himself.

This is the boy's life at school age. What, then, is school?

School is the endeavour to make the pupil conscious of the essential nature of all things and of himself. It is the endeavour to teach him the relationships which exist within the material world and which link that world and himself to the ground of all being. The purpose of teaching is to give the pupil such insight and to show him how to apply this in life and action.

School first confronts the pupil with the external world and with his own self—for he is a part of that world—as something separate and distinct. Then it shows how individual entities are connected and goes on to establish general intellectual concepts. When the boy enters school his view of the world is no longer that of external impression but of inner meaning into which he gains knowledge and insight. It is this widening of view that makes him a pupil and that constitutes the school.

It is not the getting of a greater or less amount of varied knowledge which makes a school but the living spirit which animates all things—a point which all those who direct or manage schools should keep in mind. The school implies the presence of an intelligent mind which is conscious of and involved in both the outer world and the world of the pupil and which establishes communication between them. Such a mind has mastery of this art of mediation. The schoolmaster's function is to point out and make intelligible the inner spiritual nature of things. This is what every pupil expects of his schoolmaster, and this expectation forms an invisible but potent bond between them. It was probably this which enabled our old schoolmasters to exert a far greater influence than the schoolteachers of today who merely impart information.

It may be objected that, even if this higher view of the school is true and such an ideal institution can exist, it is very difficult to point to an example, certainly not the sort of school where a tailor sits enthroned on his worktable while the children below recite their ABC, or an old woodcutter in a dark room in winter drives in the explanation of the small Lutheran catechism as he does his wedge in wood-splitting. But that is just the place where it may exist. How otherwise could the blind show the way to the lame? Only because the child has faith that his schoolmaster will show him life's inward unity and significance. The schoolmaster achieves what he does only by virtue of this faith. This turns the stones he gives the children into bread—if not for the head, yet for the heart. Spacious schoolrooms are, of course, a blessing but they alone are not enough. It is his anticipation and hope that make the school, even the small smoky room, dear to the child. All the great effects of such schools are the result of the faith and trust which the child himself brings. He comes into school with the hope that here he will be taught something which he cannot learn elsewhere, that here the hunger of his mind and heart will be satisfied.

The fact that boys can be mischievous in school is no contradiction of this. The school should stimulate them to greater freedom; they ought to be full of life and vigour in both mind and body, and it may be that in their high spirits they will forget the possible consequences of their actions.

It is quite wrong to think that man's inherent powers are intensified with advancing years and training. It is actually an extension and diversification which occurs, and this often tends to kill an appreciation of the earlier potentialities. We often make great mistakes in our dealings with children and take away the true foundation of their lives if we confuse these two essentially different manifestations of power.

We now trust too little to the dynamic growth of the boy's mind and let his powers atrophy. Or we merely play with his powers as they are manifested. So we treat him like a magnet which we leave unused or which we misuse; power is inevitably diminished or lost. In judging and estimating children's power we should never forget the words of one of our greatest writers— it is a far greater step from the baby to the child who can speak than from a schoolboy to a Newton. Man's later ability to extend and diversify his knowledge and insight should not overshadow our view into the earlier concentration of his power.

It is the spirit alone which makes the school a school and the room a schoolroom—not the ever deeper analysis of separate subjects but their coherence, as will be established if attention is directed to their inherent unity. Never forget that the function of a school is not to teach and communicate many things but to bring out the unity which inheres in all. It is because this is so often disregarded that there are now so many schoolteachers and so few schoolmasters, so many teaching institutions and so few schools.

It may be that the spirit which pervades the genuine school is disappearing because it has not been clearly appreciated, for even the real schoolmaster, absorbed in his vocation, may not have recognised or defined it. So we see yet again that through ignorance we may lose our greatest blessings. Children do indeed show us the right way in their intuitive hope and trust, but we must adopt it with conscious insight and deliberate choice.

Man is meant to achieve consciousness and to act freely and of his own volition.

As we consider what a school should be we see that, if instruction is not to be a mere game without effect on mind and heart, the boy must be instructed in the nature as well as the content of subjects.

We can now answer the questions—Are schools necessary? Why do we need them? What should they be like?

We should become thoughtful and efficient men, developing our powers of perception, knowing ourselves in our feelings and experiences. We should first endeavour to develop our inherent power and express the divine in our lives. We should grow in wisdom and understanding of the human and the divine. We should know that we and all other earthly things are a temple of the living God. We should know that we are to be perfect even as our Father in heaven is perfect and live our lives in the light of this knowledge. It is the purpose and justification of a school that it leads us to this knowledge.

What should the school teach? To answer this question we have to observe boys and their needs at this stage of their development.

We see that the boy is convinced of the existence of a spiritual self and has a vague intuition that it is caused and conditioned by a higher spiritual being on which all things depend. He feels that this spirit encompasses all. He seems to be involved in an effort to make more and more explicit his understanding of his own spiritual nature, and to confirm his intuition of the spiritual nature of all things. In approaching the world which confronts him he has the feeling that it is animated by a spirit like that which animates himself, and he longs to become conscious of his possession of this spirit—a longing which recurs whenever he responds with wonder to the natural changes of days and seasons.

The outer world confronts him as conditioned and made either by human needs and powers or by the force that is at work in Nature. Between this outer world of form and substance and the inner world of mind and spirit appears a third world—that of language—which at first was to him an element of both but of which he is now aware as a separate but mediating force.

So the mind and the outer world, and language as the connection between them, are the pivots of the boy's life. Through them the school and its system of instruction should lead him to know first himself and human nature in all its relationships, secondly God as the eternal ground of all being, and thirdly Nature and the outer world as caused and conditioned by the eternal spirit. The school should lead him to a life which accords with such knowledge, and so enable him to progress from a vague preference for it to a deliberate and enduring acceptance, and then it will be possible for him to reach his fulfilment on earth.

The endeavour to make explicit our intuition that man's spiritual self is in origin one with God and the effort to achieve union with God and maintain this union unimpaired in every condition and relationship of life are religion. This perception of a spiritual self which rests in and proceeds from God is stimulated and strengthened by religious instruction. Such instruction makes known the qualities and nature of the soul which is conditional on God, whose essential being and activity it also reveals. It gives understanding of God's relationship with man, clearly shown in the life of each individual and in the scriptural history of mankind. It applies this knowledge to life in general, so that the divine may be expressed in the human and man may know his duty and achieve his essential aim. It shows how the endeavour to live in unity with God may be satisfied, and how this relationship may be restored if it is broken. It can have an effective influence only in so far as it already finds in the mind a real sense of religion, however vague and indefinite. If it were possible for a human being to exist without a sense of religion, nothing could give it to him.

Man rarely achieves clear insight into the nature of religion, simple as it is and inherent in his own nature. Since he himself has a material existence, he bases his conception of unification on the idea of unity in space and time, and he assumes that separation must precede unity. Yet God, eternally developing from himself, remains forever one and undivided. True fundamental unity does not imply that separation has occurred—indeed it positively rules it out—nor does unification either suppose or require that a union must happen in space and time. . .

If the human being recognises that his spiritual self came from God and was originally one with him and that in consequence he is continuously dependent on God and in perpetual communion with him, if he recognises that his well-being lies in this dependence, and if he constantly acts upon this knowledge, he truly knows God as his father. If he knows himself to be a child of God and lives in accordance with this knowledge, this is the Christian religion.

The only key to an understanding of the connection between the divine and the human is the discernment of spiritual relationships between human beings. Only in the degree to which we discern such relationships and are true to them shall we reach full insight into the connection between God and man. We do not yet know, we have not the least idea of what is so near to us, one with our own life and self. We do not even live up to the knowledge and intuition which we so proudly profess, as is daily shown by our behaviour towards our parents and children and by our attitude to education. We wish to be children of God and are not yet sons to our parents; we wish God to be our father but we are far from being fathers to our children; we want to have insight into the divine but we have no regard for the human which leads us to it. Insight into the connection between God and man and full understanding of it is a manifold blessing, based on a living relationship between parent and child. We think of humanity as static, set limits to it, and consider that it has already reached full development; but it exists only in and through progression and is not something to be moulded over and over again in its present form. We do not know our own nature and the nature of mankind, yet wish for knowledge of God and Jesus. We do not know God because of our belief that we know all there is to know about ourselves. Though we want to come to God, we separate him from man, but we should realise that every apparent separation implies an original inner unity...

Every human being as a creature whose life came from and continues to exist in God should come to the religion of Jesus. Every school should first of all teach the Christian religion.

Nature gives expression to the assertions of religion and confirms the truths which contemplation of God teaches. It fulfils the demands of religion, for, like everything that exists, it is a manifestation and revelation of God.

The relationship of Nature to God can be understood by analogy with that of a genuine work of art to the artist...In the work of art there is no material part of the artist's being, yet his whole spirit is present in the sense that it lives and is expressed there and is in this form communicated to others in whom it lives and grows. As the human spirit is in this way related to the work which it produces, so God's spirit is related to Nature and all created things. It is in Nature that God's spirit lives and works; it is here that it is expressed, communicated and developed. Yet Nature is not the body of God.

The work of art is the product of the artist's entire spirit; when it has gone out from him, as it were, it has an independent existence, yet is still at one with his spirit. So God's spirit, having issued from him, lives on and acts in Nature independently, yet is still at one with him. Nature is not the body of God, nor does God dwell there as in a house; his spirit lives in Nature and supports, protects and fosters it. Even the merely human spirit of the artist lives in his work, continuing to inform and sustain it.

Great artistic achievement, even when it is in ruins, can inspire succeeding generations with the signs of vanished power and greatness. If a work of art is destroyed man sorrows almost more than if an ordinary existence had ended. If a work of art can affect entire generations, what must Nature, the work of God, be to man? We make an effort to understand man's work, and rightly so. Our effort to recognise the meaning of God's work should be all the greater. The works of Nature are everywhere for us to study. In them more easily than in the works of man we can distinguish general truths and discern the divine spirit. We can see imaged there man's dignity and greatness and the limitations and forms under which he can achieve his destiny. Nothing is more instructive than the life of plants and trees where we can see clear evidence of the workings of inner life.

If we seek the reason for the deep symbolic significance of the various phenomena of Nature in their relation to man, particularly in the correspondence of their phases of growth, we shall see that it is based simply on the fact that Nature and man originate in one and the same eternal being and develop according to the same laws, only in different stages of progression.

If Nature and man are compared and considered in the light of mankind's general development, then they explain each other. Through understanding the causative and creative connection between his mind and the work he produces man gains insight into the causative, creative spirit of God and of Nature, which is God's work, and he comes to know how the finite springs from the infinite, the material from the spiritual.

Not all man's works are the production of his hands; form and shape can be created by the will, the decisive glance, or the spoken word. Although apparently a finite being, man can out of insubstantiality produce and shape material substance, as is seen if one analyses the sequence of development from the most insubstantial thought to its clearest definition in the written word. So man can come to an understanding of the difficult process by which the material proceeds from the spiritual and, in consequence of the emergence of his own individual thoughts into outward form, can know it in his own thinking not as a concept but as a fact...

So the human being, especially in boyhood, should

become closely acquainted with Nature, not merely with the details and forms of its phenomena but with the divine spirit which is contained within it. This the boy deeply feels and needs. Where this sense of Nature is still unspoilt, nothing unites teacher and pupil so closely as a common effort to study its phenomena. Teachers should regularly take their classes out of doors—not driving them out like a flock of sheep or leading them as if they were a company of soldiers, but walking with them as a father with his sons or a brother with his brothers and making them more familiar with whatever Nature or the season offers.

To the objection that schoolchildren in the country are out of doors all day long I reply that this does not mean that they live in and with Nature. Many adults as well as children treat Nature as one ordinarily treats the air: one lives in it while knowing almost nothing about it. Children who spend all their time in the open air may still observe nothing of the beauties of Nature and their influence on the human heart. Yet—and this is the important point—the boy sees in his mind the significance of the life of Nature around him, but if he does not find the same awareness among adults the seed of knowledge just beginning to germinate within him is crushed. He rightly requires adults to confirm his perceptions, and if this does not happen he suppresses his original feelings. This is why it is important that boys and adults should go out and strive together to absorb the life and spirit of Nature and let it influence them.

Nature confronts the contemplative mind, as it has always confronted it, in the totality of its being and effect, in its essence as the entire image and word of God. So it expresses, communicates and awakens God's spirit in and through its totality. However, its appearance to the ordinary observer is entirely different. He sees it as a multiplicity of separate and isolated things, each with its own special form and purpose. To him there is no sign that all these outwardly separate units are organically connected parts of a great, living, natural organism, an intrinsically and spiritually coherent whole, and that Nature itself is such a whole...

All the various forms of Nature are conditional on one source of energy, and all stages of their development result from it. In origin this energy is a single force operating in each individual entity, but we first see it in all the multiplicity of form—a multiplicity which it implies. Here again is confirmation of the truth that everything fully expresses its nature only in a three-fold process of unity, individuality and diversity. The transformation of crystals from simple to multiple form is an example of the general mode of natural development. In the evolution of earthly beings man is the last and most fully formed. In him there is the highest equilibrium and symmetry of physical form; in him the original power which is the eternal appears as living spirit. So man discovers and understands the power that is in him. But there are forces—appetites, desires and passions—that surge and flow in his mind which can be compared with the energies that surge and flow in the worlds of natural phenomena. So he will find that a knowledge of these worlds is important in his education. Nature in all its diversity must be shown to the boy as one great living whole, as a unity in continual evolution. The boy cannot be satisfactorily instructed in natural history, as it is called, unless he comes to know the unity which causes all the diversity of natural activity and form. All observation which is fragmented and unrelated, as contrasted with a study of particular objects such as establishes their unity, deprives Nature of living meaning, and deadens the enquiring mind.

These few suggestions on the study of Nature will have to suffice here. They are intended only as a guide to the father or teacher as he leads the boy to see Nature as a living organism and to know both the uniformity of law which exists in its various phases of growth and also the unity which is contained in all its diversity. We have indicated the interconnection of natural processes in general terms only. So the pupil needs to be shown Nature in all its aspects—form, energy, substance, sound and colour.

Father and son, teacher and pupil, parent and child walk always in one great living universe. The teacher or parent should never say that he knows nothing of all this. It is not a question of communicating knowledge already acquired but of calling forth new knowledge. He needs to observe for himself and reflect on his observations, and guide the child to do the same.

In order to know the universality of law and the unity that is within Nature, there is no need of technical terms but only of precise interpretation and accurate description. Natural objects should be presented to the boy in such a way that their properties can be perceived and their distinct characteristics studied and described. Teachers should not conclude that they have no knowledge of natural phenomena because they do not know the terms; they can learn far more from observation than from reading the usual books. The so-called higher learning is usually based on observations which the simplest person is in a position to make, if he knows how to use his eyes; he can easily make observations better than those achieved by the costliest equipment, provided that he will study continuously and accept the guidance of the young people around him.

Parents need not think that they cannot teach their children because they themselves know nothing; this may be so, but it is no great evil if they are willing to learn. You should become a child with the child and let yourself learn, as he does, from Nature who is our mother and from the fatherly spirit of God manifested there. How otherwise does anyone begin to teach?... You should be guided by the boy's unerring eye and mind. If you follow his questions both you and he will learn from them. It is true that children ask questions that no one can answer. Either they take you to the limit of earthly knowledge and the threshold of the divine—in which case you should tell the child and he will be satisfied in his mind—or they merely surpass your own knowledge and experience, and this you must admit, being careful not to speak as if the limits of your knowledge were those of mankind's, for this would stunt his mind's growth. You and he must seek to understand the problem together and find an answer, and this will happen if you examine the life of your mind and compare it with the life around you, for you will see God clearly revealed in all his works.

Among Nature's great diversity man seeks a constant factor if he is to know its inner coherence. What can be a better starting point than mathematics, which seems to be the source of all multiplicity, yet is also the visible expression of all conformity to law and of law as such? So it has always been called the science of cognition because it has this quality of absolute comprehensiveness.

Mathematics mediates between Nature and man, since its laws are inherent both in the world of thought

149   10-3

and in the world of phenomena. It is possible to study Nature directly in her forms and organisms and through the laws of thought formulated in mathematics. Therefore mathematics mediates, engenders and conditions knowledge. It is not self-contained, a fixed sum of isolated truths fortuitously discovered, but a living whole, continuously evolving as the human mind gains ever greater knowledge of the unity and diversity of the universe. It is not something set apart from real life but an expression of life as such. It appears to progress from diversity of phenomena, yet it always has reference to a remote inner unity. All mathematical forms must be regarded as essentially interconnected, conditioned by the unitary principle contained in the sphere and the circle. Although instruction must begin with individual and diverse figures, these must always be referred to this all-pervading unity.

Mathematics is the expression of spatial conditions and properties. In space there is diversity of direction, shape and dimension; but number, form and size must really be a threefold unity. Number expresses multiplicity and the varied directions of energy, and so it is the product of living laws which are based on the very nature of energy. Size and form can only be explained through multiplicity, and a knowledge of number is the first essential. Number is the basis of a general knowledge of space, but space itself is not static; it exists only through the constant action of energy which is conditioned on existence as such. As space itself results from and is conditioned by the primal cause of existence, so the general laws of space underlie all spatial phenomena and even the laws of thought and knowledge themselves.

Mathematics should be treated far more as a study of

physical and dynamic factors and as a product of Nature and energy. Then it will become more instructive and useful than we have yet imagined not only for knowledge of Nature, especially in its chemical, i.e. material, structure, but also for knowledge of the character and functioning of man's mind.

The education of man without mathematics, or at least without a basic knowledge of number and some study of form and size, is a flimsy patchwork. It sets insuperable limits to the training and development which man is meant to achieve and, since he cannot rid himself of the striving which is a feature of his mind and character, this means that he either spends his energy in trying to transcend them or becomes frustrated and apathetic. For the mind of man and mathematics are as inseparable as the soul of man and religion.

What, now, is language, the third of the central points in the life of the boy and mankind? How does it relate to the other two?

Wherever there is a real relationship the pattern of unity, individuality and diversity appears. In religion it is the spiritual aspiration towards unity which is dominant. In Nature and mathematics it is primarily the intellectual demand for certainty in reference to individual phenomena. In language it is the claims of reason in its search for the unifying bond that exists among all diversity. These three are inseparably connected and have the same purpose, which is the revelation of their necessary unity.

Whatever is true of one of these applies in its appropriate form to the others. It is a fallacy that each can reach full development and be studied in isolation. In education we must know and value all three in their close and living interconnection, otherwise the school and we as educators are lost in unending multiplicity.

Language, which gives expression to the constant movement of the life of the mind, must reveal the qualities and characteristics of life. It must be flexible to the highest degree if man is to reveal his whole being in all its aspects. It also reveals the character of Nature, since man is a part of Nature. It gives a picture, therefore, of the inner and outer world of man. Since both these worlds are revelations of Divine law, language is also such a revelation...

Religion, Nature and language set the child who has been brought up simply and naturally in the centre of all life. It is difficult for him, however, to keep in mind all his varied experiences and accumulated knowledge while a still richer life is at the same time developing within his mind. As he becomes objectively aware of this world of experience he urgently feels the need to preserve his ideas and impressions in tangible form. So writing is developed.

Writing in pictures and in symbols assumes an overflowing richness of life in thought and experience. This richness gave rise to writing and only in virtue of it does the child develop a real need to write. Parents and teachers must, therefore, take care to make the life of their children's minds as rich as possible, not so much in diversity as in activity and meaning. If this is not done and if writing and learning to write are not connected with some inner need, the mother tongue becomes something extraneous, alien and lifeless, as it is now for so many people. Only if in each particular we walk again on the highroad which all humanity must tread will the freshness and vigour of man's early life return to us in and through our children. Then the potentialities and powers of the mind and the qualities of discernment and insight which are now so enfeebled will come back again in all their fullness and strength.

Why is it that we make no serious effort to walk this road again? The boy tries to lead us back to it. Here is a child painting a picture of an apple tree in which he found a nest with young birds, and there is another painting his kite flying high in the sky. In front of me a small child not yet six years old is sitting; in his book he is drawing and painting by himself pictures of many of the animals he saw yesterday in a menagerie. Surely everyone who has much to do with little children has at some time been asked for paper so that they can write a letter to a father or a brother? The boy is driven to ask because he wants to share with them what is in his mind.

It should always happen that teaching and instruction are connected with a need really felt by the boy. It is also absolutely necessary that this need should have been previously developed in a definite context before the boy can be instructed with any advantage or success. Here is a main cause of so many deficiencies in our schools and methods of instruction. We teach our children without first arousing this need and, it may be, after we have already destroyed what was in the child. How can such teaching be successful? . . .

Through the processes of writing and reading, which presuppose a certain living knowledge of language, man rises above every other known creature and draws nearer to the realisation of his purpose. In practising these arts he first attains a personal identity. It is the effort to learn to read and write which makes the boy a pupil and brings the school into existence. The ability to write enables man to achieve self-consciousness. It gives rise to true knowledge, which is self-knowledge, for he can then contemplate himself and look objectively at his own being; he can make a connection between himself and the past and future, the near and the remote. So he is enabled to reach the highest levels of his development. Writing is the first important act in the growth of free, spontaneous consciousness.

Since reading and writing are so highly important, the boy must already have sufficient power and discernment before he begins to learn them. The possibility of self-consciousness must have been awakened in him, the need to read and write must exist, and the urge, even the compulsion, to do so must have been unequivocally shown. If he is to learn them to any real purpose, he must already be a self which can become conscious, and not still be at the stage where he is seeking awareness of something that does not yet exist. Otherwise all his knowledge will be alien and imposed. If the foundation is so lifeless and mechanical, how can it give rise to that true life and activity which are the greatest prize of all our striving?

We have considered the central points of human life under three aspects. For the complete expression of man's nature we must consider also the expression of his inner life as such, which is achieved in art. All human concepts but one are relative and interdependent, showing distinctive characteristics only at the extreme levels of their development. So art has links with mathematics, language, the representation of Nature, and religion. But, if we consider it only with reference to education and aesthetic appreciation, we will have to disregard this and view it simply as representation of the mind.

It is evident that art must take various forms as the

modes and materials of expression vary—sound, lines, colours, surfaces, mass. But here again there can be countless modifications and combinations among the various forms. Expression in sound is music and song, in colours it is painting, in the forming and shaping of material it is modelling. The last two are connected by drawing or representation by line, which is therefore the link between representation by surface and by mass. The effort to draw appears at an early stage of man's development; the effort to express thoughts and feelings in shape and colour also appears early, often in childhood and certainly at the beginning of boyhood. We conclude, then, that the aesthetic sense is a general property of man and should be fostered early in the child's life. In this way he will be trained to appreciate aesthetic values, and a true education at school will show him whether or not he has the ability to be an artist.

Singing, drawing, painting and modelling at an early stage must, therefore, be taken into account in any comprehensive scheme of education; the school should treat them seriously and not consider that it is a matter of mere whim. The aim is not to make each pupil proficient in one or all of the arts—though in a sense this is true—nor to turn them all into artists, but to enable every person to develop all sides of his nature, while recognising man's abilities in their full diversity and appreciating true artistic achievement.

Poetry, like drawing though in a different respect, is also a connecting link, for it belongs both to language and, as a concise expression of the world of mind and spirit and an enduring statement of life's ebb and flow, to art. In everything, whether it is life or religion or art, the ultimate aim is the clear expression of the true nature of man.

Thus we have considered the aim and meaning of human life in its totality and indicated its expression at the level of the child in school. We have attempted to explain the purpose of the boy's aspirations and the aim of school teaching in its fundamental unity and in its relevance to the boy's whole nature.

The school must be connected with the family, for it is here that the child grows up to boyhood and school age. Today the most urgent need in education is that the school should be united with the life of home and family. This is now imperative if mankind, and in particular the German people, is at last to rid itself of the burden of ideas and concepts which are formally communicated and lifelessly memorised, and if it is to rise to living perception and real knowledge. We must stop playing games in our words and deeds and going through life in a mask. It would be well for our children and for future generations if we realised that we possess a great load of extraneous knowledge, which has been imposed on us and which we foolishly strive daily to increase, and that we have very little knowledge of our own that has originated in our own mind and grown with it. We must not pride ourselves on thoughts and feelings that are not our own. We must cease to estimate the success of our education and our schools in terms of this show of knowledge.

Must we go on stamping our children like coins instead of seeing them walk among us as the images of God?...

Mankind is meant to enjoy a range of knowledge and insight and to possess productive power such as we do not yet imagine, for who has measured the limits of humanity which is born of God? Yet this should emerge from each individual's development, growing forth in the freshness and vigour of youth, as new creations which he himself produces...

We have given an outline of the phases and conditions of human development from birth up to the first years of boyhood. We have also looked generally at the coherence and interdependence and at the various branches of those means of development which are possible and desirable for a human being during this period and which, if he is aiming at perfection, satisfy the demands both of his nature and of this phase of his existence.

If we now survey all that has been said so far on this point, we see that much appears in the boy's life which has as yet no particular or definite direction. His work with colours is not intended to make him a painter; his singing is not meant to train him as a musician. These activities are aimed primarily at the all-round development of the young human being. They are the food his spirit needs, the air in which his spirit lives as it grows in strength and scope. The qualities of mind and spirit with which God has endowed man unfold in all directions, appear in various forms, and must be met and satisfied in a variety of ways.

We should realise that we disturb a boy's nature by our interference when we repress or force the many-sided tendencies of the young and growing spirit and when, in the belief that we are serving God and man and providing for the boy's future well-being, we cut off certain of these tendencies and graft others in their place. God does not graft or implant. So there should be no engrafting of the human spirit. God develops the smallest and most imperfect things in constant progression and in accordance with eternal laws which are inherent and active within them. To be like God should be man's highest aim in all his thoughts and actions, particularly when he stands in the relationship of a father to his children as God does to men. In educating our children we should bear in mind that God's kingdom is of the spirit, and that the spiritual in man is at least a part of that kingdom. For this reason we should concentrate on the general training of the human spirit in its proper sense—as an individual manifestation of the divine—confident that everyone who has been rightly educated as a human being is trained for all the demands and needs of civil and social life.

It may be objected that this is too late for children who are already becoming adolescent and who now need to be trained for a future vocation. Yes, this may be so; but does this mean that they are to be deprived of this training for the rest of their lives? If we say that they can make up for all that when they are grown up and have leisure, we are fools. Our own nature contradicts us, if we pay attention to the meaning it conveys. It may be that here and there something—I cannot say what—may be retrieved, but deficiencies in education during the years of childhood are not generally made good. Can those of us who are parents not at least be honest? Must we hide from ourselves the never healing wounds which bleed all our life long, the calloused places in our hearts, or the dark ineradicable stains on our souls which are left when estimable thoughts and feelings are wiped away—all the result of our misdirected youth? Can we not see in our hearts all the seeds of excellence which became withered and dead at that time? Will we not do this for our children's sake? We may hold an important office, be successful in our profession or business, and take pleasure in our social refinement, but, in the moment when we confront ourselves alone, can all this spare us from the realisation of gaps and discontinuities in our education or remove the feeling of incompleteness and imperfection caused mainly by our own early education?

Therefore, if our sons are to become integrated persons, they must return to childhood if they have not learnt and developed as they should have done. This they must do, even if they are in the last years of boyhood, in order to retrieve whatever they can. They may be held back for a year or two, but it is surely far better that they gain a true objective than, at best, an illusory one.

We wish to live a full life, yet we understand so little of its real demands. We wish to be men of business and account, yet we know so very little of the business which concerns everyone, and we calculate so very poorly in matters which are of the highest importance.

We pride ourselves on being rich in experience, yet show it so little when its fruits are to be gathered. We scorn to look back and examine our own youth which could teach us so much both for ourselves and for our children, yet the demand that we turn back and examine our early years and keep eternal youth alive in our hearts is implied in the words of Jesus, 'Become as little children'. Much that Jesus said to his contemporaries is still said to us and to our age. The statements then made about the beginning of an entirely new view of life are of general application whenever the gaining of a new and higher stage of human perfection is in view, and are now reiterated afresh to all mankind. So it can now be said, 'If the spiritual demands of childhood are not fulfilled in you and your children, you will not attain your heart's desires or achieve the hopes which filled the happiest periods of your life, such hopes and desires as belong to the greatest of human beings.'

If we now put into one sentence the phases and purpose of the education achieved by the methods described in this book we can say: the boy has reached awareness of his individual spiritual self; he feels and knows himself as a spiritual whole; his ability to understand a whole as a concept both in its unity and its diversity has been aroused; he is beginning to develop his own power to express a whole both in its organic unity and in its component parts and in doing so to represent his own self in the unity and diversity of his nature.

2 Plan of an institution for the education of the poor in the canton of Berne

W. Lange, *Friedrich Fröbels gesammelte pädagogischen Schriften*, vol. I, pt. I, pp. 456–72

To Herr Schneider, President of the Society for Christian Education in Berne

Since you graciously request from me information about the nature of elementary education with particular reference to the education of the poor, I will outline my principles and views.

In the education of man, whatever else may have to be taken into account, there can be only one principle and aim—his full development as an active, sentient, understanding person; as a rational creature who creates, feels and thinks; as a being who is constantly aware of the inner unity and harmony of all spiritual things. These three apparently different aspects of his development are intrinsically one, and these phases of growth are not really separated at any point. In each and all of them he is deeply aware of a spiritual connection and of a single ground of all existence, which is of the spirit, for it has being and life in itself. Because of this man is what he is—a human being.

It is on the child's humanity that man's relationship to God as creature to creator, as part to whole, as child to father is based. Human existence is no other than a religious life, the Christian life of unity with God— God recognised as the father of men, and men as the children of God. This unity with God is a given factor in man's existence. This striving for experience of immediate fundamental relationship lies within man's being as sparks in a stone, as life in a seed; but it must be developed and cherished. The religious life is fundamental to the stage of development we have now reached and is, even at the subconscious level, the nerve centre of all human activity and thought. The aspiration for close unity with God is part of the life of man, and so it is there in the child's disposition and quickens the child's mind.

Everything which is of value in human education holds good for elementary education. Indeed, if we are to make distinctions, it is of value here most of all. Here, however, everything must be given definite form and must throughout be closely linked with life; there is no place for the lifeless concept, the empty word, the mere game of reason. In elementary education it is of particular importance that, along with the fostering of ability in the three main directions, here above all there should be an especial regard for the care of Nature and for creativity and representation in material form. This is the starting point. Even religion must be presented mainly through outer forms and in such a way that the spiritual becomes manifest through the phenomena of life.

If one examines the history of the human race, one sees that the course of its development conforms to these basic principles of education. So it can be said that education, particularly elementary education, must follow this plan, but it must do so at a high level of insight and consciousness. This must be related to man's first beginnings. The first men had nothing apart from their spirit and its awareness of the divine. Nature was to them as if it had lost its signposts—alien, desolate, hostile—as it still is to those unfortunate people who are estranged from themselves and look around only for help.

There must be constant unity with God the Creator at the level not of vague feeling but of intellectual recognition and regard, and this involves a continual effort to show both the primal cause and aim and also the living coherence of all things. This is the rock on which the house of elementary education is built. This is the seed from which the centuries-old tree must grow. The nation itself and every single member of it, even the poor, can exist only if they consciously dedicate themselves to creative activity. Each individual must do this, recognising his inner unity with the whole universe and resting in it and in himself. This is the highest principle of elementary education, and it is of particular importance if any scheme is to serve as a model for now and for the future.

Life in and with Nature is the first essential for such creative activity. First, then, the child should study the basic natural products—stones, plants and animals; he should cultivate the soil, and work in field, garden and orchard. True elementary education for the poor must first of all be based on the cultivation of the land, for here the child sees how material is transformed first in form and shape and then along the lines of its essential character; it also promotes and extends his manual skill. When the child observes Nature and cultivates the earth and its products he begins from and is led back to a consideration of God, whom he feels within him and whom he observes and recognises in the outer world. As the child engages in the activity of caring for something and causing it to grow, he is taught to find within himself the laws of formation which he can see are effective in natural phenomena. In sharing the results of their skill and industry the pupils exchange their different experiences and enlarge their knowledge and insight. So they come to strive for and desire other knowledge and skill. This, of course, varies among the pupils according to the different modes and levels of their abilities and aptitudes of both mind and body, but the most talented may perhaps go on to the higher study of an art or science.

It is clear, then, that the teaching in elementary schools, even those for the poor, may not—at least if it is to be true to its nature and principles—exclude any subject or concept which is implied by the material objects and which man can discover. So all things must be observed and affirmed in every possible way: in their way of life and their similarities and dissimilarities; in respect of material, form, size, number, shape or design, colour, sound, movement or name; in their cause, formation and effect. So also the pupil must be trained in conformity with the main directions of all his intellectual powers and the demands of his mind as instrument of the spirit, and this must be done according to his talents and abilities.

Therefore the teaching in elementary schools is differentiated from that in special and higher educational institutions not so much by the topics of instruction as by its method and levels, its range and relationships. In this teaching it is the thing, the action, life itself that is important. Here teaching and learning are based always on the object itself, and the range of the instruction is determined by the fact that it is directly concerned with life, and moreover with the life of a particular people. Yet the teaching must always be an organic whole.

This view of education gives for everyone the possibility of further development. Every potentiality at every level of development which is to be found among the nation's youth is to be encouraged, and this applies even to the children of the poor. It is, therefore, the first and most important task of all elementary education to awaken in the pupil not only his innate ability but also that spontaneous drive and keenness which is fundamental to reflection and thought. This drive is easily aroused if total and free development is permitted, for every being desires and strives to become perfectly that which it is capable of becoming; and it has the innate ability to do so. The ways and means of attaining this need to be shown, and then those who have the ability and energy will independently pursue them.

There need be no fear that individual pupils will want to improve their position and leave their own class. On the contrary, this system will produce educated men, each true to his calling, each in his own position. No creature, and certainly no man whose life is undisturbed, seeks to go beyond his powers and abilities. He wants only to perfect himself as he is, and he is completely happy when he has done so. But if, as can happen, a desire for higher education does arise, this is no cause for regret. If such an educational institution is started with a few carefully chosen, able boys, they will express their ambition in the choice of teaching as a profession. And this is all to the good, for it benefits the people and the entire state. History shows that the best popular educators have always come from the people, and almost always from the poorer class, and they have known what the people and the poor needed.

Since true elementary education is closely linked with the life of Nature, the sequence of its activities and, indeed, its whole life must be arranged in relation to the demands of each season. Through this interaction between the life of Nature and the life of man the pupil should respond to the appropriate instruction, and it is important that this period of receptiveness should be utilised. So the teacher must be in closest relationship not only with human life generally as well as with his pupils' lives but also with the whole life of Nature.

The pupil will know each thing properly and give to each sphere of activity its full significance if he comprehends it in relation to time and place and specific circumstances. It is in this way that he comes to see clearly the whole of life, and he becomes conscious of his knowledge and ability only as a result of clear and coherent thinking and observation. But this process of bringing one's own knowledge or the lack of it to the level of consciousness and this ability to see the use of one's own gifts is the aim of all education, though it is of particular importance here. It may well be that the final cause of poverty to which all else can be reduced is just this unawareness of one's own knowledge, this inability to use the gifts one has.

We can see the truth of this all around us. The aims

of the educator are already achieved by many a hard-working and contented peasant in the midst of his home and family. In all his actions, feelings, and thoughts he lives at unity with God and Nature, with man and with himself, and seeks to lead his children and grand-children in the same path, though his awareness of what he is doing is very limited.

The very real difficulties of elementary education lie in the effort to lead children to clear consciousness, to get them to appreciate their knowledge and ability, and to give them the strength and skill to use them so as to achieve true satisfaction.

The educator must also take into account children's propensity to copy in their own lives the models set before them, and this is the greatest and most effective means of influencing them at this stage. The educator's task here is to show the children the qualities of such a model life and to analyse it in its growth and influence.

In such an educational institution the results of the pupil's activities must flow into the whole, just as in a well-ordered family the satisfaction of an individual's needs has a general effect and does not stand out as an isolated success. So the things which the pupils make should not be produced for the sake of their artistic merit and no monetary reward should be given, or else the school sinks to the level of an industrial institution. The attitude which such a spirit of self-seeking induces cannot at this stage of education be endured, for it must destroy the harmony which ought to prevail. In such groups it is trust in God and childlikeness of disposition which should prevail.

In such an institution the value of skilled handwork lies in the development and training which it gives to the child in knowledge, insight and sensory experience and which are absorbed into his life and thought, and this is a process which occurs in the whole educative group. Here as elsewhere the child must work creatively in order to try out many things rather than to produce a particular object perfectly....

These results of activity must further serve to show children that what they have learnt verbally can be given material form and, conversely, that forms can rise to words, feelings and sensations can become deeds, and activity is rich in human relationships. Furthermore, the pupil learns to work more for the good of humanity, for the alleviation of the sheer physical labour that is the lot of working men; and as he makes and uses tools he gains insight into the smallest details of the objects on which he works.

Just as representational activity must be closely connected with the total life of the institution, so must play. Play, which reflects the free activity of the whole life of the pupil's mind, must give back again that which education and experience have taught him. It must always be in agreement with the child's whole life as well as with the whole of Nature—never isolated. Then it has educative significance and reveals its meaning to the child in all that he does. It is certainly true that a child who plays really hard—and I use this phrase deliberately—will also within the sphere of his abilities learn well and become capable and efficient.

Play, therefore, must not be left to chance. Just because he learns through play a child learns willingly and learns much. So play, like learning and activity, has its own definite period of time and it must not be left out of the elementary curriculum. The educator must not only guide the play, since it is so very important, but he must also often teach this sort of play in the first instance. Once children have learned the value of appropriate and lively play they very rarely want to do this sort of play unless an adult shows them and plays with them.

Physical games have a special place in such an institution, for the pupil must be trained in physical skill as well as in strength and endurance. It is not to be supposed that a child who works hard physically does not need such free activity or that, since so much physical work goes on, no organised physical exercises are useful. They cannot be left out, if only because they have a necessary inner coherence which proceeds from the simple to the complex and finally lays claim to the whole human being. In such an institution everything must be a living interlocking whole which secures and advances the interests of its members—never merely fragmented. Such fragmentation has impoverished many a people.

As such an institution has ground to cultivate and manage, so it has a place suitable for play and movement and appropriately large playgrounds. These are necessary for the pupils of the institution, but also specially important for the adults of the region since the children benefit when everyone participates in their life and play. So, in setting up an elementary and charity school, regard should be paid to the needs of adults as well as those of youth; it must have an educational value for them. If such an institution is not in close and living relationship with the people's lives, it is usually as inadequate as is the education of men away from Nature and without the influence of natural life. There must certainly be intercommunication, if only so that adults may protect children against the intrusion of evil. Yet we must do more than merely watch and prepare for the people to begin to participate in a small way.

As far as the site and character of such an institution are concerned, both must be as rural as possible. As to the site there must be a suitable large place near areas of ground sufficiently extensive, and as to the organisation it must be modelled as far as possible on that of a good and sensible countryman.

With regard to the pupils with whom such an institution would start it is certainly good that the number of pupils at the beginning should be only small, and even these should be chosen in relation to character and inclination. In public education, just as in the education of individuals, one must first of all encourage the good and hardworking, and the bad will wither away.

Such an institution must only very cautiously increase, for a healthy root must first be established before a tree can grow, and the pupils must stay there until they reach maturity of will and judgement.

To go further into details of organisation, it must be realised that the man and woman in charge of the institution cannot, any more than the father or mother of a large family, share all the pupils' activities. They must, however, carry in themselves the life of the whole, managing it with such cheerful confidence as to secure contentment and serenity. Whoever takes on this work must be content in himself and must be able to be content with his lot. The position of the housefather and housemother must from the very beginning be that of a countryman who can live without material worries if his house and means of livelihood are in good order. These are essential conditions for the success of any education, for it is clear that too much or too little can be equally harmful for creative living.

The inner life of the community must also be evident. So the pupils, as sons of the institution, should use familiar terms and Christian names in speaking to each other—otherwise even in a homogeneous group there will be disruption and division. The children should talk to their foster parents in the same way as children of the region normally talk to their parents.

On Sundays and festival days the children may wear a special form of dress, but it must be simple—nothing distinguishing or conspicuous, especially not a livery or uniform—and in line with the usual dress of the region.

Such an institution must be a community which resembles the well-organised family of a countryman or honest townsman, and so all its members must have a share in the occupations and, wherever possible, undertake all the business of the household. On each weekday there must be some time for learning (usually in the morning) and some time for work, for getting things done—and this must be arranged with some reference to the seasons. The evening is the time when preparations can be made for the next day, general household work done, and the demands of the communal life of the group met.

In a group where there is such full interchange and community of purpose individuals will in a short time be both learning and teaching each other. Also it will become more effective in the outside world and, as its own cohesion and independence develop, so it will come more into contact with the people. For this wider relationship it would be a good thing if the German language could be the language of the institution because of its formative effect on those who speak it, and also because concepts are bound up with forms of speech, and language is therefore an important factor in promoting national unity....

Such an institution must also have its festivals and holidays just as every ordinary family has. It must have its own occasions (family festivals) which serve partly to join the members of the group more closely together and partly to unite the institution as a whole community more intensely with the people.

I believe I have now in general dealt with the problem which you referred to me, but you may find my answer too far-reaching since you only asked for suggestions. My only reason for writing at length is my belief that the educator has in mind the totality of human nature and development, even when considering particular and special aims.

Although I have many times thought over this subject, I had first to live through the whole again in my mind. Also I wanted to give you evidence that the whole scheme is ever present to my mind. So you receive here much that you already know. It is my firm conviction that the present stage of human development is such that everything which happens in education at whatever level must be done in harmony with the course of Nature and of history, and with complete insight and awareness as well as with entire clarity as to means, method, aim and end, i.e. we must act with full consciousness of what we are doing.

The time for superficial experiment is over. This is true of many things, but especially of education. We are rational beings and should at last begin to act rationally, i.e. with a clear sure consciousness, and so act according to eternal laws. We must stop fumbling around and patching up even if only in the education of the poor. If we do this, then associations for Christian education will really make the poor rich in the true apostolic meaning of the word.

If you would like a word about my position here, it is just the same as I mentioned in my letter. My activity in the canton is not curtailed by any clash of opinion or parties, but it is consumed by selfish interests. Everyone wants a way of education such as I have described here, but no one is willing to seize the obvious means to achieve it. Each says that the other ought to start first. Some do make a start, for, since the examination which you know about, many look on such an institution as a good milch cow. But they want the cow not only to yield good milk and rich dung in return for poor fodder but to give a good return in stable money as well. What the cow should do in such circumstances or what will happen to her I do not know.

Willisau, 24 October 1833   *Friedrich Froebel*

CHRONOLOGICAL TABLE OF EVENTS IN FROEBEL'S LIFE

1782   April 21: born at Oberweissbach in the Thuringian forest, a village in the state of Schwarzburg-Rudolstadt.

1783   February: death of mother.

1792   Sent to uncle in Stadilm.

1797–9   Goes to Neuhof in the Thuringian forest as a forester's apprentice.

1799–1801   At Jena University.

1801–5   Various posts as land-surveyor, estate manager, official in a forest department, private secretary etc. Reads the writings of Schelling, Novalis and Arndt.

1805–7   In Frankfurt. Becomes a teacher in Gruner's model school. Visits Pestalozzi's institute at Yverdon in autumn of 1805.

1807   Becomes tutor to sons of Caroline von Holzhausen.

1808–10   Stays with pupils at Yverdon.

1810   Returns to Frankfurt.

1811   June: goes to University of Göttingen. Writes the treatise *Sphaïra*.

1812   November: goes to University of Berlin to study crystallography under Weiss.

1813   At Easter joins volunteer corps taking part in war of liberation.

1814   In July returns for brief time to Frankfurt; begins to read Boehme. In August takes up post as assistant in mineralogical museum in University of Berlin.

1816   November: establishes Universal German Educational Institution at Griesheim in Rudolstadt.

1817   Transfers school to Keilhau. Joined by Middendorff and Langethal, his wartime student companions, and, ten years later, by Barop, Middendorff's nephew.

1818   Marries Wilhelmine Hoffmeister.

1820   Begins to write articles on 'national work' of German education, some of which were published in the *Isis*.

1823   Krause's comments in the *Isis* on the Keilhau articles.

1826   *The Education of Man.*

1827   *Letter to the Duke of Meiningen.*

1828   *Letter to Krause.*

1829   Draws up plan for Duke of Meiningen for a national educational institute at Helba.

1831   Abandons the Helba project. Goes to Frankfurt and then to Wartensee in Lucerne and opens a school. In August writes *Letter to the Women in Keilhau*.

1832   Transfers school to Willisau in Lucerne.

1833   Writes *Plan of an institution for the education of the poor in the canton of Berne*.

1835–6 In charge of school and orphanage for canton of Berne at Burgdorf; establishes pre-school classes for children from the age of three.

1836   Writes *Renewal of Life*. Returns to Rudolstadt.

1837   Begins to develop series of 'gifts and occupations'. Opens an institute for the education of young children at Blankenburg.

1838–40 Publishes *Sunday Journal* in which writes articles on play material. Begins to travel to promote new movement.

1839   Death of wife.

1840   Founds German Kindergarten at Blankenburg. *Outline of a plan for founding and developing a Kindergarten*. In the following years makes several journeys to promote and establish Kindergartens, e.g. in Dresden, Darmstadt, Hamburg, Heidelberg, Frankfurt, etc.

1843   *Mutter- und Kose-Lieder.*

1848   August: attends a teachers' meeting in Rudolstadt which draws up petition to the National Assembly. Leaves Keilhau.

1849   Settles at Liebenstein near Eisenach and begins to train Kindergartners.

1850   Bertha von Marenholtz-Bülow visits institution and begins her championship of the cause. Institution is removed to Marienthal in neighbourhood of Liebenstein.

1851   August: prohibition of Kindergartens in Prussia, which was not rescinded until 1860. Marries Luise Levin.

1852   June 21: dies at Marienthal.

SELECT BIBLIOGRAPHY

There is a comprehensive list of German texts and publications in the edition by Erika Hoffmann: *Fröbel. Ausgewählte Schriften*, vol. 1. Kleine Schriften und Briefe, pp. 183–201.

1. *Froebel's chief writings*

(a) *German texts*

GUMLICH, B. (ed.). *Friedrich Fröbel. Brief an die Frauen in Keilhau* (Weimar, 1935).

HOFFMANN, E. *Fröbel. Ausgewählte Schriften* (Dusseldorf, 1951, 1961). Vol. 1: Kleine Schriften und Briefe; vol. 11: Menschenerziehung.

LANGE, W. *Friedrich Fröbels gesammelte pädagogische Schriften* (Berlin, 1862–3). Vol. 1, pt. 1: Aus Fröbels Leben und erstem Streben; vol. 1, pt. 2: Ideen Friedrich Fröbels über die Menschenerziehung; vol. 11: Die Pädagogik des Kindergartens.

SEIDEL, F. *Friedrich Fröbels pädagogische Schriften* (Vienna and Leipzig, 1883). Vol. 1: Menschen-Erziehung; vol. 11: Das Kindergartenwesen; vol. 111: Mutter- und Kose-Lieder.

(b) *English translations*

FLETCHER, S. S. F. & WELTON, J. *Froebel's chief writings on education*, rendered into English (London, 1912).

HAILMANN, W. N. *Education of Man*, an abridged translation (New York, 1887; New York and London, 1912).

HERFORD, W. H. *The Student's Froebel*, 2 parts (London, 1893–4, 1911–15).

JARVIS, J. *The Education of Man* (New York, 1885).

—— *Pedagogics of the Kindergarten* (New York, 1895).

—— *Education by Development* (New York, 1899).

LORD, F. & E. *Mother's Songs, Games and Stories*. Froebel's *Mutter- und Kose-Lieder* rendered in English (London, 1885).

MICHAELIS, E. & MOORE, H. K. *Autobiography of Friedrich Froebel*, translated and annotated (London, 1886). [This consists of selections from the *Letter to the Duke of Meiningen* and the *Letter to Krause*.]

—— *Froebel's Letters on the Kindergarten*, translated from the *Kindergarten-Briefe* (1887), ed. H. Pösche (London, 1891).

2. *Comment and criticism*

BLOW, S. E. *Symbolic Education* (New York, 1898).

DEWEY, J. 'Froebel's Educational Principles,' *The Elementary School Record*, no. 5, June 1900. (Chicago, 1900.)

JUDGES, A. V. *Freedom: Froebel's Vision and our Reality* (London, 1953).

KILPATRICK, W. H. *Froebel's Kindergarten Principles* (New York, 1916).

LAWRENCE, E. M. (ed.). *Friedrich Froebel and English Education* (London, 1952).

McCALLISTER, W. J. *The Growth of Freedom in Education*, ch. xx (London, 1931).

MACVANNEL, J. A. *The Educational Theories of Herbart and Froebel* (Teachers' College, Columbia University, Contributions to Education, No. 4, New York, 1905).

MARENHOLTZ-BÜLOW, BARONESS BERTHA MARIA VON. *Reminiscences of Friedrich Froebel*, translated by M. Mann (London: Cambridge, Mass., 1877).

MURRAY, E. R. *Froebel as a Pioneer in Modern Psychology* (London, 1914).

SPRANGER, E. 'Aus Friedrich Fröbels Gedankenwelt', *Abhandlungen der Preussischen Akademie der Wissenschaften*, Jahr. 1939. Phil.-hist. Klasse, Nr. 7 (Berlin, 1939).

WALLAS, GRAHAM. *Men and Ideas*, ed. M. Wallas (London, 1940), pp. 133–50. Address to Froebel Society, Jan. 1901, 'Criticism of Froebelian Pedagogy'.

INDEX